Abstraction Mechanisms and Language Design

ACM Distinguished Dissertations
1982

Abstraction Mechanisms and Language Design,
by Paul N. Hilfinger

Formal Specification of Interactive Graphics Programming Languages,
by William R. Mallgren

Algorithmic Program Debugging,
by Ehud Y. Shapiro

Abstraction Mechanisms and Language Design

Paul N. Hilfinger

The MIT Press
Cambridge, Massachusetts
London, England

Second printing, 1986

This book was printed and bound in the United States of America.

Publisher's note: This format is intended to reduce the cost of publishing certain works in book form and to shorten the gap between editorial preparation and final publication. Detailed editing and composition have been avoided by photographing the text of this book directly from the author's typescript or word-processor output.

Dissertation submitted to the Department of Computer Science, Carnegie-Mellon University, June 1981. The thesis research was sponsored by the Defense Advanced Research Projects Agency (DOD), ARPA Order No. 3597, monitored by the Air Force Avionics Laboratory under Contract F33615-78-C-1551, and by the National Science Foundation, Grant No. MCS-7703883. The views and conclusions contained in this document are those of the author and should not be interpreted as representing the official policies, either expressed or implied, of the Defense Advanced Research Projects Agency, the National Science Foundation, or the US Government.

Library of Congress Cataloging in Publication Data

Hilfinger, Paul N.
Abstraction mechanisms and language design.

(ACM distinguished dissertations)
Originally presented as the author's thesis—
Carnegie-Mellon University, 1981.
Bibliography: p.
Includes index.
1. Programming languages (Electronic computers)
I. Title. II. Series.
QA76.7.H54 1983 001.64′24 82–25899
ISBN 0–262–08134–2

Series Foreword

The Distinguished Doctoral Dissertation Series is a welcome outgrowth of ACM's annual contest, co-sponsored by The MIT Press, for the best doctoral dissertation in computer-related science and engineering.

During the judging process that is designed to select the annual winner, it has inevitably developed that some of the theses being considered in the final round are of such high quality that they also deserve publication. This book is one of those dissertations. In the judgment of the ACM selection committee and The MIT Press, it truly deserves special recognition as a Distinguished Doctoral Dissertation.

Dr. Paul Hilfinger wrote his thesis on "Abstraction Mechanisms and Language Design" while at Carnegie-Mellon University. The thesis work was supervised by Professor Mary Shaw, and the thesis was submitted for the 1982 competition. The Doctoral Dissertation Award committee of ACM recommended its publication on the grounds of its impact on the Ada language design and its lucid presentation of design principles. It is both a scholarly and a pragmatic addition to the growing literature on Ada.

Walter M. Carlson
Chairman, ACM Awards Committee

Acknowledgments

I would like to thank my committee—Mary Shaw, Bill Wulf, Nico Habermann, and Steven Fenves—for their helpful comments on drafts of this thesis. It is a particularly great pleasure to thank Mary Shaw, my advisor lo these many years, and Bill Wulf, of equally long acquaintance, for the pleasure of their collaboration and for their unfailing support, advice, and encouragement. Andy Hisgen and Jim Saxe provided many useful comments on previous versions of the work that makes up this thesis. Jean Ichbiah, Olivier Roubine, and the other members of the Ada language design team, besides their obvious contribution of providing me with subject matter, also helped to make my stay in France a pleasant one. This document was produced using the Scribe system developed by Brian Reid, to whose Martin Luther I have had the pleasure of playing Philip Melancthon. I would like to thank the Computer Science faculty for putting up with me for longer than I had any right to expect, and I suppose that I should say the same thing of the department as a whole.

Finally, and perhaps most importantly, I am greatly indebted to many people for keeping me sane during my graduate years: my students, the current and former residents of 2 Olympia Place, the members of the Pittsburgh Camerata and the Pittsburgh Savoyards, Guy Almes, and Philip Long.

Table of Contents

List of Figures

Abstraction Mechanisms and Language Design

Chapter 1
Definitional Mechanisms

Programming languages are notational systems that facilitate programming. They do so by providing concise notations for some set of useful functions, state operators, and control structures (which are essentially functions on functions and state operators), together with facilities for defining new notation. We call these latter features *definitional mechanisms* or *abstraction mechanisms*. For example, FORTRAN provides notation for standard arithmetic and trigonometric functions, an assignment operator, I/O operators, and control structures for composition of operators (sequential execution), conditional branching, bounded iteration, and, of course, the notorious `go to`. Its abstraction mechanisms include the ability to declare variables, which are abstractions of state data, and routines, which are new state operators and functions.

At first, FORTRAN's variable and routine definition were about the only abstraction mechanisms to be found in the commonly-used von Neumann languages[1]. Later, languages such as Pascal, Algol W, and Algol 68 introduced definitional mechanisms for data structures. The newest von

---

[1]The term "von Neumann language" is due to John Backus, who used it in his Turing Award Lecture [Backus 78] to describe languages that, like most conventional programming languages, have state-transition semantics and fairly primitive data domains (what Backus calls "word-at-a-time" processing). I will use the term to refer to any blatantly non-applicative or statement-oriented language. Thus, it includes FORTRAN, the Algol family, PL/1, Pascal, Ada, COBOL, BLISS, and so forth. I specifically do not include Lisp in this list, even in its impure forms, because of Lisp's more powerful primitive data structures and its strong expression orientation.

Neumann languages—dating back to Simula and including experimental languages such as Alphard, CLU, and Euclid—include more elaborate mechanisms for defining data *types*, which are entities comprising data structures and operations and control structures over those data structures.

This recent attention to abstraction mechanisms in von Neumann languages stemmed from the methodological turmoil that followed the recognition of the "software crisis" in the late 1960's. Data type abstraction, encapsulation facilities, and the like were seen as devices for organizing complex systems—for separating systems into semi-autonomous modules that present to each other relatively simple interfaces, abstractions of their functions, while hiding details of representation that are irrelevant to these abstract functions.

In addition, abstraction facilities provide a convenient tool for defining a programming language. The ultimate example (still) is probably Lisp, whose primitive data type is so powerful that it serves to implement abstraction mechanisms that must be built into other languages. As a result, the basic Lisp system is extremely simple to define and implement, and it serves as the kernel of several extensive programming environments, among them Maclisp and Interlisp, which are nearly indispensable to the AI community.

This trend toward increased abstraction capability, however, is by no means universal. First, users of common von Neumann languages are usually sufficiently concerned about the time and space costs of their programs that they are unwilling to accept the costs typically associated with "high-level" abstraction mechanisms. Indeed, even something as simple and traditional as the subroutine call with parameters in FORTRAN is sufficiently costly in some implementations, or at least is perceived to be, that programmers will endure rather ugly alternatives to its use (such as arcane COMMON blocks). Second, the full power of definitional mechanisms to assist in defining a language environment remains unexploited. The particular example of interest here is Ada [Honeywell 80], which has been criticized for its size; it has extensive definitional capabilities, but to a large extent, they are added on to a conglomeration of features, rather than being used as a framework in which to cast or define these features.

This thesis considers the design of abstraction facilities in von Neumann languages. It has two principal themes. First, proper design of the abstraction facilities of a language not only increases its utility to programmers, but can also simplify the language and reduce the language designer's temptation or need to provide all things to all programmers. Second, the benefits of abstraction mechanisms to programmers and language designers need not involve substantial performance costs. These statements are "folk knowledge" among many programmers, but they have yet to be acted upon on any large scale; most production work is done in FORTRAN or COBOL—languages with very primitive definitional capabilities.

It is the nature of language design in general that it cannot be convincingly discussed without a concrete example. The bulk of this thesis, therefore, is cast in terms of the design of a particular von Neumann language intended for production use: Ada. First, we will look at how principles of abstraction affected its design between its preliminary and revised versions. The analysis presented in the next two chapters describes work that I did on revising the Preliminary Ada language. Several of my recommendations, as discussed in those chapters, were eventually adopted in Revised Ada. Second, we will see how further applications of abstraction could improve Ada's current design. To begin with, however, we will begin by deriving some general criteria to be used in designing a language.

1.1 Purposes of a Programming Notation

Wulf has listed three roles for a programming language [Wulf 80a]:

- A design tool

- A device for human communication

- A vehicle for instructing a computer

For fulfilling these roles, high-level programming languages provide at least the following important aids:

- Expressiveness: High-level programming languages provide a natural and concise notation for expressing algorithms. A "natural" notation reflects the notations and concepts associated with the problem at hand, or at least provides a set of concepts in which it is easy to model them.

- Documentation: This might also be called "expressiveness of intent"—the ability of the programmer to assert things about his program.

- Consistency checking: The other side of documentation is the ability to assure that it is observed.

- Freedom from detail: The notation should allow the programmer to suppress details that are locally irrelevant. Part of this is what I'll call "incrementality"—the programmer's ability to build on previous work (ignoring its details) and to separate work into sections.

Let's consider these in a little more detail.

1.1.1 Expressiveness

The FORTRAN language was named after what was expected to be its primary use: FORmula TRANslator. The scientific programmers who were its initial audience dealt with algorithms expressed with algebraic formulae, and were hampered by the need to translate these into sequences of register loads and stores, arithmetic operations, and the like. The expression language provided by FORTRAN narrowed the gap between the concepts and notations used in the statement and analysis of a problem and the notation used to describe the desired computation. Narrowing this gap accomplished several things:

- It speeded up the programming process. There was less translation to do and FORTRAN source code—like the formulae it was used to express—was typically shorter than the corresponding object code.

- It facilitated reading a program. Understanding a mathematics package, for example, amounts to re-constructing the mathematics involved. The less reconstruction (de-compilation from the source program, if you will) there is, the less effort for the reader.

- It reduced chances for error.

Algebraic expressions are by no means the only place where the expressiveness of a high-level notation is useful. A set of arrays in FORTRAN can represent a recursive tree structure, for example. The hardships in doing so, however, are familiar (as for example when it comes time to write a tree literal). The list notation and primitives provided by Lisp, or the pointer types and structure literals provided by Algol 68, greatly facilitate the manipulation of such structures.

It is important to distinguish expressiveness—the availability of notation—from functionality—the availability of effects. One can use arrays in FORTRAN to get the *effect* of pointers, but at considerable notational (at least) inconvenience. The failure to distinguish expressiveness and functionality creates considerable confusion in debates about programing languages. Very often, we tend to say, "You can't do X in language Y" rather than, "You can't do X like this in language Y." Our natural bias toward familiar ways of doing business often causes us to miss reformulations of our problems or methods that bring them within the purview of an unfamiliar (or perhaps I should say, rival) programming language.

1.1.2 Documentation and consistency checking

The obvious example of documentation is the comment. However, the declaration of variables' types or subranges falls in the same category. Likewise, the declaration of the types of the parameters of a subprogram is a form of documentation. The specification part of a package in Ada can serve as the syntactic specification of a data type[2].

Documentation serves several purposes:

- To communicate with the readers of a program (including the author).

- To assist debugging by allowing the inclusion of redundant information about argument values or program state, information which the language system can check for compliance. The static type-checking rules of many Pascal systems are examples, as is the checking of subranges.

---

[2] That is, as the specification of a domain of values and of the names and functional types of the operations and constants defined for it. See, for example, Wulf et al. [Wulf 80b].

- To provide information to the translator that allows the production of specialized (optimized) object code. A classic example is the use of subrange data provided in Pascal to suppress index bounds checks.

1.1.3 Freedom from detail

To invoke an arithmetic operator from a high-level language, a programmer does not need to know its operation code or register usage. To access a variable he does not need to know its address. To invoke a subprogram, he does not need to know its body. We say that the variable is an abstraction of the physical memory location or that the subprogram name is an abstraction of the body. Indeed, the primary use for abstraction mechanisms is in freeing us from these and other details.

One important detail from which a programmer should be freed is the generation of good object code, by which I mean object code that achieves reasonable costs in code and representation size and in speed, relative to some theoretical optimum *for the intended effect*. This last qualification turns out to be crucial. For example, the LISP expression `(PLUS X Y)` requires considerable evaluation time for checking the bindings of `X`, `Y`, and `PLUS`, and the types of their values. This is not necessarily "inefficiency," but it is potentially inefficient if the programmer intends that `X` and `Y` always be bound to integer values and that `PLUS` always be bound to the arithmetic addition operator on small integers.

The term "information hiding," introduced by Parnas [Parnas 71], is often used to mean the ability to keep details of an implementation from a user of the facility implemented. In fact, the important criterion is not what a programmer *cannot* do or know, but rather what he *need not* do or know[3]. Object code efficiency provides a prime example. Some people may believe that the purpose of an optimizing compiler[4] is to produce fast code. More importantly, however, it relieves the programmer from having to worry about the quality of object code his compiler is producing and about what circumlocutions he should be using to trick it into "doing the right thing." Speaking from the point of view of the programmer who implements a certain facility, the important criterion is the degree to which a language allows him to put details where he wants them to be. As an example of how a language might not, there is an implementation of Pascal that allows separate compilation of groups of subprograms, but also requires any user of such a separately-compiled group to repeat their headers—and any type definitions required to specify them—in his program. Furthermore, the implementation in question does not check the correctness of the repeated headers. Without the aid of an additional tool (a pre-processor, for example), the definer of this group cannot take on the responsibility of providing this detail.

One important form or property of information hiding is what I've called *incrementality*. I use the word to refer to the ability to build on or use previous definitions without having to re-build the definition. Given a piece of program text that performs some function, how much must a programmer know or say to invoke this function? A related question that one may ask about a language: What functions or specifications *can* be embodied in some centralized piece of text? For example, a FORTRAN subroutine allows one to take an arbitrary operation on some global state data and invoke it using a

---

[3]Or in other words, "It is impossible to design a language that prevents bad programming and harmful to try."

[4]That is the common term. I prefer (and will use) the term "production-quality compiler" elsewhere.

single name. On the other hand, FORTRAN does not allow one to encapsulate the fact that, for example, two particular variables compose a single record and are always to be passed together as a unit in procedure calls and the like; FORTRAN has few provisions for data structuring.

1.2 Approaches to providing "high-level" power

We can divide the approaches taken to fulfilling the purposes of a programming notation into two camps: those that concentrate on rich, pre-defined environments, and those that concentrate on a set of tools for producing such environments. Let's start with the first.

Until fairly recently, programming languages concentrated on expressiveness and freedom from very low-level detail. Assembly language was an advance over machine language because operator mnemonics were (to a human) more evocative than octal constants, as were symbolic addresses. FORTRAN provided a notation resembling algebra. APL added linear algebra and tensor calculus. SNOBOL introduced strings and text patterns.

All of the languages just mentioned are instances of the "semantic stew" school of programming language design. The (unstated) theory is that from a rich enough supply of standard operations, a programmer will be able to quickly assemble concise solutions to his problems. In languages where the stew is particularly meaty, such as APL and SNOBOL, the definitional facilities can be quite scanty. In languages such as Algol 60 and FORTRAN, the definitional facility stops with variable and procedure definitions. The languages Algol 68 and Pascal added definitions for *data structures*—for representations of objects composed of simpler objects by a small set of constructors.

1.2.1 Definitional Approach

In contrast to the typical semantic stew, the LISP universe is rather primitive. LISP provides little more than a notation for function application and definition, plus a very few primitive operations. However, because of the power of its primitive value domain—which serves to model LISP programs themselves—the ability to define functions suffices for defining new data and control structures as well. A typical LISP implementation (such as MacLisp) provides a large quantity of semantic stew, but with all of it expressed in the same uniform notational framework, and, indeed, definable from the base kernel of the language.

Similarly, the paper languages Alphard and Tartan [Wulf 76, Shaw 78] were originally conceived to be notational frameworks within which the programmer could both specify and implement new extensions to the facilities provided by the languages, given an arbitrary set of primitive types or modules to begin with. Alphard even went so far as to posit a single underlying type corresponding to blocks of primary memory.

The advantages of these approaches should be clear. They provide an underlying regularity of notation and a small initial set of notions which are easy to understand and implement. This in turn provides a base from which other features of the language may be defined. In other words, there can be a clear separation between a simple language kernel and the standard environments (sets of useful definitions) that are built using this kernel. One language kernel can serve many different environments, and this relieves the language designer from much of the burden of being all things to all people. For example, Jean Ichbiah, the principal designer of the Ada language, has publicly refused to discuss or defend the standard I/O package documented in the reference manual [Honeywell 80], on the grounds that since it is a library package, a programmer or installation is free to replace it, without thereby generating a new version of Ada. In other words, I/O is not a "language issue" in Ada as it is in PL/1 or FORTRAN.

Another advantage of the definitional approach, when it is properly carried out, is that the language designer needn't be pre-emptive. A language that provided no facilities for defining subprograms—that pre-empted the decision of what routines were available to programmers—would be obliged to provide a sufficient set of built-in subprograms for all applications. This is an impossible task unless the language is intended for a very limited range of applications. A similar comment applies to data structures. As Shaw and Wulf discuss in a recent note on language design [Shaw 80], pre-empting the programmer's ability to define can lead to circumlocution and inefficiency, which discourage the use of high-level languages.

1.2.2 Problems with the Definitional Approach

The advantages of the definitional approach seem so clear that one might wonder why it is not universally adopted. The problem appears to be one of performance. A program written in a language such as LISP is generally slower than or more space-consuming than a computationally equivalent program written in, say, Pascal. The reason for this is basically that because the primitives of Pascal are much more specialized than those of LISP (an integer is a special form of atom; a record is a special form of list), a Pascal compiler has much more information about its programs, and can thus generate much more specific code than is (conveniently) possible in LISP.

The problem is that the LISP notation is not as expressive of the programmer's intent or assumptions as is the Pascal notation and *not* that LISP is "too general" or "too high-level." However, one enduring piece of folk wisdom is that high-level definitional features of the sort LISP offers are to be avoided because they must necessarily lead to "inefficiency." This folk wisdom was reflected, for example, in the STEELMAN requirements document [DoD 78], which forbade functional values in the DOD-1 language, and in the repeated pleas of conservatism found throughout the Rationale for GREEN [Ichbiah 79a] as justification for restrictions in the language.

1.3 Criteria for Evaluating Definitional Facilities

In evaluating the abstraction mechanisms of the various versions of Ada that we will consider (preliminary, revised, and proposed), we must keep in mind the various facilities of high-level languages listed in Section 1.1. We can extract from them several desiderata for the definitional mechanisms of a programing language.

- Expressiveness: The mechanism should support (allow the definition of) familiar or natural notation for describing the computations to be performed.

- Freedom from detail: The definitional mechanism should allow a programmer to protect his clients from details of the implementation of any definition he writes and should support incrementality. What the client must do to use some abstraction should depend as little as possible on the way that abstraction is implemented. Likewise, the definer of an abstraction should be protected from the details of his clients.

- Expressiveness of intent: The programmer must be able to supply the compiler with enough data that the latter can produce object code that is no more general than necessary. In popular parlance, this would probably be phrased "no less efficient than necessary." It amounts to the same thing. At the same time, however, the programmer should not be unnecessarily burdened with having to express his intent, either for the purpose of satisfying the language semantics or for obtaining adequate object code performance. This is mostly a requirement on compilers for the language, but a language design should not make the process unduly difficult.

- Simplicity: On general principles, the definitional kernel should be reasonably simple in the sense that concepts do not proliferate unnecessarily. In particular, the language should get as much mileage as possible out of its definitional mechanism, never introducing something as a distinct language construct which can better be explained in terms of the definitional mechanism.

The criterion of simplicity, in particular, deserves some special discussion because it is often misunderstood. It is clear that *gratuitous* complexity in a programming language is undesirable. An elaborate mechanism for abbreviating keywords, for example, probably buys very little but to expand compilers' tables. However, it is *not* the case that "the smaller the better." Consider the Turing Machine, which is surely the simplest general model of computation available. Its very simplicity is its biggest problem. The facilities it provides are so limited that not only must a programmer generate volumes of state transitions to accomplish the simplest task, and not only can't he easily compose solutions to parts of a problem into a complete solution, but the performance of the machine inherently suffers by at least a factor of the size of working storage over conventional RAM machines. The moral is that a simple language avails nothing if programs written in it are inherently complex by dint of its simplicity[5]. Indeed, I'll even propose the radical suggestion that because a language's semantics are a fixed target, the size of the language is not as important as its expressive power; a language's expressive power is what determines how easily it adapts to a new application.

---

[5]Shaw studies the related problem of how the presence of features affects compilation costs [Shaw 74]. The trade-off there is that adding a feature to a language will increase the overhead costs of compilation, but may reduce total cost by decreasing the size of source programs.

1.4 Thesis

The discussion in the remaining chapters uses a concrete example of a language design to demonstrate the relative advantages of a sophisticated set of abstraction mechanisms and to show that the current state of the art in languages and compilers allows us to realize these advantages within the confines of a production language. I use the Ada language—both in its Preliminary and Revised versions—as the concrete vehicle of study, concentrating mainly on ways in which the design, at various stages, could be (or was) improved by some adjustment to its definitional mechanisms. In particular, I'll consider

- Redundancies in the design: places where features were added that were already adequately handled by other abstraction facilities;

- Unnecessary compromises: places where abstraction power was lost in the mistaken belief that compromise was necessary for performance reasons;

- Unfortunate gaps: places where a relatively simple addition to the abstraction facilities would have simplified the language or the task of programming in it;

- Performance traps: places where an abstraction mechanism was inadvertently rendered costly by some overlooked side-effect of the design, and places where the task of compilation could be simplified by allowing greater expression of intent.

Chapters 2 and 3 are essentially revised versions of Language Issue Reports that I submitted on Preliminary Ada. It was as a result of these reports that I was invited to join the Ada language design team during early 1980 to help make certain revisions, as detailed in those chapters. Chapter

4 continues with comments on Revised Ada. Each of these discussions tries to demonstrate ways in which improvements to the definitional facilities of Ada can improve the language—increasing its regularity and its utility to programmers—without introducing distributed overheads that endanger Ada's use as a "production" language.

1.5 Background

The Ada language was the result of a competitive design effort sponsored by the Department of Defense. Carlson's article [Carlson 80], which serves as source for the statistics in this section, contains a full description of the procurement effort and its background. After the final selection, in the spring of 1979, there was an extensive review of the preliminary language design, resulting in over five hundred "language issue reports"—essentially analyses problems and requests for changes—from over a hundred organizations.

I submitted two of the early reports [Hilfinger 79a, Hilfinger 79b], which contained critiques of the type system and the tasking facility. These form the basis of the next two chapters. There were, in fact, quite a few areas of the language that needed work. However, the two areas I chose both contained distinctive and fundamental semantic features of the language. Tasking in particular received a great deal of attention throughout the review, because of its novelty.

The major changes between Preliminary and Revised Ada involved types, tasking, generics. A large portion of the changes to the former two consisted of the substance of the two reports cited, and I served as a consultant to the language design team while it incorporated these changes. In looking back on this experience, I realized that my initial analysis had, in fact, largely been the result of applying the general principles expounded in this chapter. The rest of this thesis attempts to demonstrate this application.

Chapter 2
Abstraction Issues in the Type Mechanism of Preliminary Ada

This chapter discusses issues involving the abstraction facilities provided by the typing mechanism in Preliminary Ada (PAda hereafter). Perhaps the most influential requirement placed upon the Ada design was that it allow an implementation that would satisfy its clients' desire for "efficiency." That is, the community of reviewers and potential users effectively required that the object code produced by an Ada compiler, as well as the representations used for the program data, be at least comparable to what an assembly language programmer (or a good FORTRAN compiler) would produce. For the purposes of this thesis, I will for the most part simply accept this constraint and examine its consequences, tempting though it is to contest its appropriateness in some cases.

Thus, the Steelman document [DoD 78] requires that Ada be "strongly typed" in the sense that "the type of each variable, array and record component, expression, function and parameter shall be determinable during translation." Of course, in a trivial sense, this property applies to most languages—by this rule, an implementation language such as BLISS is strongly typed, having exactly the one type `word`. The intentions behind the Steelman requirement were apparently twofold:

- First, there should be a useful and extensible set of classifications of variables and values corresponding to their intended use in a program—as numbers, tables, switches, etc.

- Second, this classification should obviate dynamic determination of representation. That is, the object code produced for an operation should not need to include any discrimination on the representation of its operands. Likewise, the representations themselves should not need to include hidden tags identifying themselves.

These two criteria are somewhat at odds, of course. Thus, one might distinguish two enumeration types because they serve different purposes, even though they have identical representations as small integers. Likewise, one cannot directly define a type modeling inhomogeneous lists—lists that contain items of arbitrarily mixed types. Section B.2 discusses this last problem and indicates how other facilities of Ada partially alleviate it.

One particular problem with the second criterion, well-known to serious Pascal programmers, arises with types whose objects, conceptually speaking, can have different "sizes." For example, in Pascal[6] one can define

```
type String1 = packed array [1 .. Max1] of char;
     String2 = packed array [1 .. Max2] of char;
```

where `Max1` and `Max2` are previously-defined constants, but one cannot define a single type embodying "strings of any length" without abandoning array representations altogether.

Ada provides facilities for making just such declarations. In PAda, however, these facilities were formulated in a way that unnecessarily restricted the programmer's ability to define useful data types. Section 2.1 reviews the relevant portions of the design of PAda's type. Section 2.2 goes on to present an analysis that I made of problems with the design. This analysis led to the revisions that are reviewed in Section 2.3.

---

[6] This applies to Pascal as described by Jensen and Wirth [Jensen 74]. The newest revision of Pascal [Addyman 80] has a feature for allowing array formals without constant bounds.

2.1 Type parameterization in Preliminary Ada

Consider a type VString1 that is supposed to capture the notion of a string of characters. We can imagine several possible semantics for such a type. For example, for a given variable of type VString1, there might be no restriction on the length of string that it can contain. The minimal specification of such a type could contain simply some primitive coercions to and from the pre-defined type STRING[7]:

```
package Strings1 is
   type VString1 is private;

   function Conv(s: STRING) return VString1;
   function Conv(v: VString1) return STRING;
      -- For all s:STRING, v:VString1,
      --    Conv(Conv(s)) = s;  Conv(Conv(v)) = v.
end Strings1;
```

Now it should be clear that such a specification requires the equivalent of dynamically allocated storage for its implementation. For example, if the programmer should know that a particular VString1 will never be longer than 10 characters, he cannot convey this information directly to the compiler. Thus, either the compiler must forego taking advantage of such information (which would otherwise allow a simpler representation) or must deduce it. The desire to avoid both of these alternatives led, in PAda, to the introduction of a facility for imposing simple *constraints* or *parameters* upon types.

PAda provided three ways by which a user may define constraints on a new data type. First, any type derived from a numeric type is automatically parameterized by range constraints (i.e., constraints on the maximum and minimum value of a variable, parameter, or expression) and possibly by precision constraints (i.e., constraints on minimum significance or accuracy).

---

[7] Variables of type STRING must be constrained with an index constraint when they are allocated, so that may contain only values of some fixed length. Hence, the type STRING is more primitive than the type VString1.

Second, any user-defined array type automatically had an index constraint defined for it. Thus, after[8]

```
type Vector is array (NATURAL range <>) of INTEGER range 0..100;
```

one may declare

```
x: Vector(1..1000);
z: Vector(1 .. n);      -- where n may be a variable
```

In effect, the type `Vector` is parameterized.

The final type parameterization mechanism—and the main topic of this section—is that of discriminant constraints in records. In PAda, a discriminant was a constant field of a record upon which some other field depended. For example, after

```
type VString2 is
   record
      Max: constant NATURAL range 1 .. MAX_STRING;
      Len: INTEGER range 0 .. MAX_STRING;
      Data: array (1..Len) of CHARACTER;
   end record;
```

one could declare

```
Line: VString2(1000);
InLine: VString2(n+2);
```

The values `1000` and `n+2` were taken to constrain the values of the `Max` fields to those particular values (computed at run-time.) Again, in effect, `VString2` was parameterized.

One might think that this final parameterization mechanism would provide a fairly general facility for defining constraints. However, the definition of PAda stated, in section 3.7.1 of the PAda Reference Manual (PRM, hereafter [Ichbiah 79b]), that "the only permissible dependencies between record components are the dependencies of an array bound and of a variant on a discriminant." Hence, the declaration

---

[8] Throughout the discussion of PAda, I will use Revised Ada syntax as if it applied also to PAda in those places where the differences are purely syntactic.

```
type VarInt is
   record
      Max:   constant NATURAL;
      Val:   range 1..Max;
   end record;
```

was illegal (the component `Max` appears as a range constraint), as was

```
type TwoString is
   record
      Len1, Len2: constant NATURAL;
      S1: VString2(Len1);
      S2: VString2(Len2);
   end record;
```

(the components `Len1` and `Len2` appear as discriminant constraints. `VString2` is as above).

Thus, dynamic parameterization in PAda (i.e., in which parameter values may be supplied at run time) was limited to those cases in which, traditionally, programmers expect to find the parameters stored in the representation—dope vectors for arrays and tags for variant records.

2.2 Problems with the Preliminary Ada design

PAda's rules for the use of discriminants within records gave rise to three classes of problem:

- Problems in type composition,
- Problems with program structure and name management, and
- Problems in efficient implementation.

We can trace the first two problems directly to a failure to recognize discriminant constraints as a definitional tool, a generalization of the built-in parameterizations allowed for pre-defined types. The last problem, by contrast, is due to a sort of *over-generalization,* a failure to allow the compiler to make certain useful assumptions.

2.2.1 Type composition and representation hiding

The rules governing discriminant constraints in PAda provide two examples of a language's failure to properly support the programmer's ability to free his users from detail. Perhaps the most obvious problem here was the inability to encapsulate types with discriminants. A type such as `VString2` in the preceding section could not be made private, revealing just the maximum length, `Max`, without also revealing the particular choices made about representing the current length and contents. (The discriminant `Max` would have to be visible in order to properly allocate variables of type `VString2`. Even though this extraneous information is present, however, at least a user of `VString2`s can ignore it. This can't be said of our second instance of failure to free from detail.

If `T` is a type, then objects of type `T` may easily be composed using the standard type constructors **array**, **record**, and **access**. Unfortunately, any constraint parameters of `T` do not fare quite so well. Thus, one cannot achieve the effect—which was possible in the competing language RED [Nestor 79]—of

```
TYPE TwoString(n: INT):
    RECORD [ S1, S2: VString2(n) ];
```

without either reconstructing `VString2`, as in

```
type TwoString is
   record
      Len: constant NATURAL;
      S1, S2: array (1..Len) of CHARACTER;
   end record;
```

or introducing a new type (generically) for each size of `TwoString`, as in

```
generic n: NATURAL;
package StringPack is
   type TwoString is
      record
         S1,S2: VString2(n);
      end record;
         . . .
```

The first alternative leads to loss of abstraction power. In particular, any operations defined on VString2s do not carry over to the components of TwoStrings. The details of VString2's implementation may not be hidden from the definer of TwoString, to use the criteria discussed in section 1.3. The second alternative leads to severe naming problems in some cases, as shown in the next section.

2.2.2 Program structure and name management

The purpose of having parameterization of types is to increase expressiveness—conciseness and naturalness of use. It is natural to think of the operation of summing the elements of a vector, for example, as being the same operation regardless of the size of the vector. Ada's generic mechanism allows the composition of types, as shown above. Unfortunately, it exacts a price, namely that each different set of parameter values leads to a new type. The resulting lack of expressiveness makes generic parameters an unsuitable alternative to type parameterization.

Thus, after

```
package String10 is new StringPack(10);
package String100 is new StringPack(100);
```

String10.TwoString and String100.TwoString are two distinct and totally unrelated types. This can present serious difficulties. Suppose, for example, that we wish to define a function Bracket that operates on TwoStrings of any two sizes. The problem is that the operands of Bracket are of different types. One solution is to make the comparison operator generic, that is to write

```
generic  type S1type;
         type S2type;
         ?;
function Bracket(x: S1type; y: S2type) return BOOLEAN . . .
```

where "?" is replaced by whatever operations on S1types and S2types are needed to effect the comparison. Presumably, the generic parameters to Bracket will come from instantiations of StringPack. There is no way to guarantee this, however, so that Bracket is "too generic" in some sense. The programmer must explicitly instantiate Bracket for all pairs of sizes of TwoString to be compared—a non-trivial annoyance (especially to the programmer who knows that the compiler is going to use the same code!).

Nor does trouble end there. Suppose that packages A and B both use instantiations of the generic StringPack. The types of TwoString thereby derived are, of course, distinct. A third package, C, which uses A and B, cannot pass TwoStrings generated by A to routines of B and vice-versa. One possible solution would be to make A and B generic in a type and then have them instantiated by C:

```
package C is
   package MyString is new StringPack(10);
   package CA is new A(MyString);
   package CB is new B(MyString);
      . . .
```

(I am assuming that A and B are separately compiled; otherwise, of course, I would simply include them in C at the points shown and avoid the problem). Again, however, A and B are "too generic", and the possibilities for separate compilation seem to be reduced or the difficulties of deducing the possibility increased. Furthermore, the generic parameter lists of both A and B are likely to be rather bulky.

A better solution is to make a separate module, D, that looks like this:

```
with StringPack;
package D is
   package OurString is new StringPack(10)
end D;
```

Now D may be included in the visibility lists of A, B, and C. Unfortunately, this solution does not work if the bounds for StringPack are to be determined dynamically, unless we forego separate compilability (one cannot export anything from a block.)

The TwoString example is, of course, somewhat artificial. However, it would be wrong to think that this sort of composition would never occur in practice or that programmers ought to be discouraged from its use. Note that the situation differs from that of a generic body parameterized only by scalars, for example, in which the compiler might very easily discover chances for sharing code bodies.

In all of the cases discussed so far, PAda's lack of subtype parameterization has forced somewhat clumsy solutions. Such problems are inherent when one makes objects that are conceptually different-sized instances of a given type into objects of distinct types. This was one motivation for having subtype parameters in the first place.

2.2.3 Efficiency issues

Chapter 1 used the term "expressiveness of intent" to refer to the programmer's ability to convey useful information to the compiler about what assumptions it could make, and to do so easily (without having to write too much or to drop into assembly language). To the extent that a compiler cannot make assumptions, it is forced to produce general-case object code, which is liable to be relatively bulky or slow. PAda's parameter passing mechanism provides an example. Here, the compiler could not assume that certain actual parameters were or were not constrained, with the effects discussed below.

The semantics of parameter passing in Ada are that the passing of parameters is non-deterministicly by value or by reference. Proper style, therefore, is to write programs that do not depend upon the mechanism used. One way to do so, for example, is to follow the aliasing restrictions imposed by Euclid [Lampson 77].

Actually, the statement of parameter semantics above is somewhat misleading. The real desire was to have pass-by-value semantics uniformly. On the other hand, it is often desirable to pass "large" objects by reference in the implementation. Therefore, the language semantics state, in effect, that the original object may serve as its own copy. Unfortunately, the semantics of record discriminants in PAda made it impossible, in practice, to use the by-reference mechanism.

To see this clearly, consider the following set of declarations:

```
type TwoSize is
   record
      Switch: constant BOOLEAN;
      case Switch of
         when TRUE  =>  S1: array (1..5) of NATURAL;
         when FALSE =>  S2: array (1..1000) of NATURAL;
      end case;
   end record;
procedure Assign(x: in out TwoSize) is
   begin
      x := (Switch => FALSE,  S2 => ...);
      x := (Switch => TRUE,   S1 => ...);
   end Assign;
b: TwoSize(Switch => TRUE);
```

According to the PAda language definition, the call `Assign(b)` is legal and causes no exceptions during elaboration. This is because

- x is defined to act as a local variable with subtype `TwoSize` (i.e., it is unconstrained) within the body of `Assign`,

- Since x has no constraints, both of the assignments to it are legal, just as they would have been had x been a local variable declared

  ```
  x: TwoSize := b;
  ```

- The assignments to and from the actuals are legal (in particular, the constraint on b is satisfied at the time of procedure exit.)

It should be obvious that the compiler cannot pass b by reference if it also optimizes b by allocating only enough space for `S1`. Since it is important to provide this optimization, the compiler is forced to produce a copy of b (i.e., which provides adequate space for the case where the `Switch` field is true). Exactly the same comment applies to records containing dynamic arrays, since assignment to the record may change the bounds on the array unless the record is properly constrained.

It is instructive (and suggestive) to see why it is that array types themselves, which may also appear unconstrained in formal parameter lists, do not suffer the same problems. If one declares

```
type AnySize is array (NATURAL range <>) of NATURAL;
procedure Assign2(x: in out AnySize) is
   begin
      x := (1,2,3,4,5,6);
      x := (7,8,9);
   end Assign2;
```

Then the declaration

```
b: AnySize;
```

is defined to be illegal; the index must be constrained. Furthermore, any call on `Assign2` will cause an exception, since the index constraint of any variable may not be changed. The net effect is that a by-reference implementation works perfectly, and the reason is that the compiler may always count on array parameters being constrained.

2.3 Summary of revisions from Preliminary Ada

To correct the problems discussed above, the design team (of which I was by that time a member) made several revisions to PAda that I had suggested earlier [Hilfinger 79a]. In Revised Ada,

- Discriminants of records are explicit parameters of the record type rather than constant fields. For example,

```
type R(N: INTEGER) is
   record
      Len: INTEGER;  Val: array (1 .. N) of CHARACTER;
   end record;
```

- Private types may be parameterized, as in

```
type T(N: INTEGER) is private;
```

The parameters correspond to discriminants in the representation.

- Discriminants (parameters) may appear as discriminant or index constraints on fields of a record.

The first two changes directly address the problems raised in sections 2.2.1 and 2.2.2. The representation of types having discriminants may be hidden in revised Ada and the discriminants of private types may be constrained without knowing the representation of the type. Furthermore, the last change supports incrementality: one may freely imbed a component of a user-defined type with a variable size in a record.

The implementation difficulties with parameter passing in PAda, discussed in section 2.2.3, were a result of a failure to provide enough information to the compiler. That is, the compiler and run-time support were not allowed to assume any constraints upon an unconstrained formal. I had suggested that discriminant values on a formal parameter be required to remain fixed, which allows by-reference passing of records, but requires that their discriminants be set before being passed to any subprogram. Somewhat surprisingly, the design team chose instead the rule

- An unconstrained formal parameter of a type with discriminants is constrained during an invocation iff the actual is constrained. The attribute inquiry `CONSTRAINED` allows the program to find out if a particular parameter is constrained during a given call.

I say "surprisingly" because this requires passing the information that a certain parameter is constrained—the sort of thing that the design team had seemed reluctant to countenance previously. However, the semantics chosen solves the problem just as well, since it allows the compiler to assume that a constrained actual corresponds to a constrained formal, which again allows a by-reference implementation.

2.3.1 Aside: Non-Hierarchical Variants

One advantage of having dynamic record components is that it allows the definition of non-hierarchical variant records. Suppose that I have a record type, `Desc`, with a variant clause having discriminant Tag, which can take on values 1, 2, or 3. Suppose that I want

- The field `Len` to be present of `Tag` is 1 or 2,
- The field `Offset` to be present if `Tag` is 2 or 3,
- The field `Kind` to be present if `Tag` is 3,
- The field `Align` to be present if `Tag` is 1.

This is a non-hierarchical variant; it cannot be coded in the form given unless I choose multiple names for one or more of the fields (depending on `Tag`) or give up having overlapping storage. In the presence of dynamic record components, however, the problem vanishes, as shown in Fig. 2-1.

Now the `Len` field of `x`, for example, is always referenced `x.F1.Len`. There is an annoying extra field name interposed, but the desired effect is achieved. Optimizations discussed below will assure, furthermore, that only one `Tag` field will be stored in each `Desc`. Of course, the ideal would be to allow overlapping labels in the variant part, and to have the compiler decide an ideal storage layout. This puts quite a burden on the compiler, however, and the solution above is, I think, an acceptable compromise.

```
type TagType is range 1..3;
type V1(Tag: TagType) is
   record
      case Tag of
         when 1..2 =>
            Len: LenType;
         when 3 =>
            Kind: KindType;
      end case;
   end record;
type V2(Tag: TagType) is
   record
      case Tag of
         when 1 =>
            Align: AlignType;
         when 2..3 =>
            Offset: OffsetType;
      end case;
   end record;
type Desc(Tag: TagType) is
   record
      F1: V1(Tag);
      F2: V2(Tag);
   end record;
x: Desc;
```

Figure 2-1: Hierarchical variants in Revised Ada

2.4 Implementation

One part of justifying the changes to PAda discussed in section 2.3 is showing that they do not result in over-generality—that no distributed overhead is introduced. Fear of such overheads was the reason for the restrictive (one is tempted to say bizarre) rules for discriminant constraints in PAda. Here we demonstrate that there are no such overheads by considering the implementation in detail.

Ada has consistently attempted to adhere to two principles in its design:

- The principle of least surprise: the programmer should be able to predict the costs of the constructs he uses and the data structures he creates. If a clever compiler makes his guess a bit conservative, so much the better, as long as it does not make things worse.

- The single representation principle: the accessing algorithms for components of a record should be as simple as possible; there should be little or no "interpretive" code that conditionally chooses an algorithm based on subtype, for example. This is a corollary of the principle of least surprise. In Ada, one expects the compiler to choose one layout for each type at type declaration time. As a result, such strategies as call-by-reference for passing large aggregates become easy.

One naive approach would be to make all discriminants actually be fields in the record. This adheres to the principle of least surprise, since the programmer can see exactly what goes into his records. Clearly, if this naive approach is used, it makes no difference whether discriminants can be used as constraints on record types; the same amount of space is used.

Let me make this point in another way. Suppose that I had declared

```
type Inner(n: T) is
   record
      -- other fields depending on n
   end record;
type Outer(m: T) is
   record
      X,Y: Inner(m);
   end record;
```

In PAda, the closest one could come to this effect without reconstructing the type `Inner` was

```
type Outer2 is
   record
      m: constant T;
      X,Y: Inner;    -- I.e., unconstrained
   end record;
```

(which allocates the maximum space necessary to hold an `Inner`). As a consequence of the design of Ada, the compiler would always have the option of compiling records with dynamic record components in exactly this way, although one would hope that a production compiler would do better. In effect, the introduction of more general type parameterization merely gives the programmer the ability to express more dependencies within his records. Adding such information can only improve the code produced.

Before going on to discuss less naive implementations, it is appropriate to mention an important class of optimizations on record representations. Suppose that we declare

```
type D(Len: INTEGER range 1..Last) is
   record
      S1, S2: T(Len);
   end record;
```

where T is some parameterized type. Under the naive approach, it is necessary to have at least two copies of the value of Len stored in the record —one for each of S1 and S2. Note that it is not necessary to have three copies of Len. The compiler ought to be free to allocate the field Len to lie on top of one of the copies within S1 or S2.

Of course, the first question one must ask when there are multiple copies of a value lying around is whether these copies are guaranteed to be consistent. Fortunately, the designers of Ada were careful to insure that the language rules did indeed guarantee this consistency. Thus, it is impossible the change a discriminant without a complete record copy. But a complete record copy, of course, will change any copies of a value. Furthermore, in the example above of the definition of D, the fields S1 and S2 cannot be assigned except from T's with the same constraint. The combined effect is to insure the consistency of any copies of a discriminant value.

Certain optimizations are possible when discriminants are known to always be constrained, as is true of discriminants without a default value in revised Ada. Let us divide all records into two portions:

- A constraint portion that contains all constrained discriminants, and
- A data portion that contains everything else (including unconstrained discriminants).

To pass a record parameter, one passes both portions separately (because the constraint portion is constant, it is always possible to pass it by reference). To assign to a record, one assigns to the data portion alone. It is not necessary to pass the discriminant portion to any routine whose formal is a completely constrained subtype. Note, in passing, that there is one curious example of this optimization in the case where S1 is not simply a T(Len), but an array of them instead. In this case, the compiler may feel free to overlay the Len field on any of the copies within the array.

In a subtype declaration such as

```
subtype Q is T(5,7);
```

the compiler would build a single constraint portion for all variables of subtype Q. Note that this implies that the constrained discriminant fields would not have to appear in the records themselves . In a nested declaration such as

```
type Z(n: NATURAL) is
   record
         V: T(n);
   end record;
```

the constraint portion for V would be embedded in the constraint portions for the containing record of type Z. Indeed, the n field would probably be overlaid on the constraint portion for V. In a case such as

```
type Y(n: NATURAL := 10) is   -- Can be unconstrained.
   record
         V: T(n);
   end record;
```

the constraint portion for V would be part of the data portion of each Y, since it could be changed by assignments to Y. These last two cases, by the way, are simply generalizations of the various cases for T being an array type.

Finally, for access types, the constraint portions of dynamically allocated records would probably be prefixed to their data portions.

2.4.1 Handling Variants

Variant records may either be considered a problem or an opportunity for optimization, depending on one's point of view. Pascal was designed to place all variant portions of a record at the end of the record. The advantage, of course, is that all variant tags may be constrained and minimum space allocated without affecting the offset of any field . The only time that this property is not preserved in Revised Ada and PAda is when a record contains a dynamic array (or more accurately, when it contains a dynamic array plus a variant part or plus another dynamic array). In such cases, one expects that the compiler will allocate the variable-sized pieces at the end of the record and that the offsets of their bases will be stored in a descriptor (as a sort of "implied discriminant"). In the case of arrays, this offset can be conveniently added into the virtual origin of the array.

Dynamic record components would provide another source of variable-sized embedded components. Obviously, one could use exactly the same strategy as outlined above for arrays in those cases where the size of a record depends on the values of its discriminants. Indeed, an array is a sort of giant variant record.

It is important to emphasize that Pascal achieved no advantage in efficiency by constraining record structure in the way it did. In Pascal, one can still embed variant records within other records. Pascal simply provides no way in which these embedded records might have their variant tags constrained, so that compilers are forced to allocate maximum space to all of them. Ada allows (but does not force) the programmer to constrain the variant tags of these embedded components.

If one allowed dynamic record components, a naive implementation could simply do what Pascal does now—no space optimization. As one can get this effect in Ada as it stands (by not putting constraints on the embedded fields), it is merely a question of how much better a smart compiler might do with the extra dependency information.

I have already mentioned that treating dynamic records as one would treat dynamic arrays allows packing (at the compiler's option—this is a good place for a pragma). In addition, note that one useful optimization is that of overlaying identical constraint portions. This comes up most notably in the case of non-hierarchical variants (see section 2.3.1), where it allows a record to contain a single tag field.

2.4.2 Implementation summary

The addition of a more general type parameterization mechanism to PAda, while significantly enhancing its definitional capabilities, did not result in any serious implementation costs. The use of type parameters never causes surprising overheads (and in general, in fact, we may expect the programmer to be pleasantly surprised). Restricting the use of discriminants to index bounds and variant tags, as in PAda, appears to allow no significant optimizations. At worst, a compiler can use a naive implementation and achieve precisely the space efficiency available now. The investment of a little time in the allocation algorithm, furthermore, will yield considerable improvement. That is, a compiler need not be particularly sophisticated to make use of the strategies described in this section.

2.4.3 An example

As an example of the techniques we've been discussing, let's look at how the compiler could represent some parameterized types.

Consider the definitions

```
type StringInd is range 1..MAX_STRING;
type MString is array (StringInd range <>) of CHARACTER;
type TwoString(Len1,Len2: StringInd) is
   record
      S1: MString(Len1);
      S2: MString(Len2);
   end record;
y1,y2: TwoString(Len1 => 10, Len2 => n);
```

Let us assume that array descriptors for `MStrings` have the form

```
type MString_Constraint is
   record
      Multiplier, Base_Offset, Bound1, Bound2: INTEGER;
   end record;
```

From the discussion above, a compiler would implement these type definitions with the following representation declarations:

```
type TwoString_Constraint is
   record
      Len1, Len2: StringInd;
      Desc1, Desc2: MString_Constraint;
   end record;
for TwoString_Constraint use
   record
      Len1 at Desc1.Len'POSITION+Desc1'POSITION range . . .
      Len2 at Desc2.Len'POSITION+Desc2'POSITION range . . .
   end record;
        --Illegal Ada, of course, but this is merely intended
        --to be illustrative.
type TwoString_Data is
   record
      -- Data for two strings
   end record;
```

Together, `y1` and `y2` need only one `TwoString_Constraint`. The declarations (in quasi-Ada) are

```
y1,y2: TwoString_Data;
y_Constraint: constant TwoString_Constraint := ( ... );
for y1 use 10+n;     -- Size of length 10 string +
for y2 use 10+n;     -- length n string.
```

Note the most important point here: the representation of a `TwoString` takes up exactly as much space as a pair of arrays. All of the dynamic record data has collapsed into the (necessary) array descriptors.

Now consider the declaration

```
type QString(Len: StringInd := 1) is
   record   -- All discriminants unconstrained
      Data: MString(1..Len);
   end record;
```

A `QString` has no constraint portion. Its representation contains the constraint portion for the embedded dynamic array.

```
type QString is
   record
      Len: StringInd;
      Data_Constraint: MString_Constraint;
      Data: MString_Data;
   end record;
for QString use
   record
      Len at Data_Constraint.Bound2'POSITION
             + Data_Constraint'POSITION range ...;
       . . .
   end record;
```

Chapter 3
Abstraction Issues in Preliminary Ada Tasking

This chapter considers the PAda task as an abstraction mechanism. In essence, we will see first how in PAda, the role of tasks as shared data objects was unnecessarily subjugated to their role as processing elements and how this affected the programmer. Second, we will see how certain design decisions involving tasks made it difficult to hide certain details of an implementation from its clients.

Both PAda and Revised Ada provide a single mechanism for multi-tasking that resembles Hoare's Communicating Sequential Processes (CSP) [Hoare 78], simultaneously providing

1. *Processes*: routines that exploit physical parallelism or logical asynchronousness. Examples include interrupt handlers and traditional processes (in the sense of most modern operating systems).

2. *Monitors* of shared data: sets of routines that service requests from multiple tasks to perform operations on shared data objects, and that explicitly control the order of servicing requests so as to maintain the logical consistency of the data. Examples include mailboxes and shared data bases[9].

---

[9]For an introduction to monitors, see Hoare's article [Hoare 74]. We'll use the term a little freely in this chapter to indicate an Ada task whose primary function is to control access by other tasks to the data it contains, and that has no substantial processing to do outside the bodies of `accept` statements.

The Ada task provides both of these services. As a result, Ada is among the first "production" languages to promote a high-level model of concurrent programming.

PAda had several problems in its detailed realization of this model.

1. Awkwardness: the choice of the "task family" formulation of task template led programmers into a Turing Tarpit in which problems with simple solutions in "traditional" systems had only convoluted and obscure solutions in PAda[10]. This was a significant lack of expressiveness.

2. Inability to hide information: explicit initiation, the implicit global join of tasks at block exit, and the behavior of the **abort** statement and the `FAILURE` exception all made it difficult to hide the use of tasks in implementations.

3. Efficiency: in several ways, the language design forced unnecessary run-time overheads.

To motivate some of the discussion to follow, Section 3.1 discusses the use of Ada tasks as monitors. Section 3.1.2 gives a preliminary discussion of implementation techniques that make it feasible, as far as efficiency is concerned, to use the same mechanism for protecting shared data as for achieving parallel processing. Section 3.2 then discusses the problems mentioned above in detail and Section 3.3 discusses how the changes adopted in Revised Ada address these problems. Finally, Section 3.5 discusses a few issues in the implementation of tasks in Revised Ada that result from the revisions.

---

[10] The term "Turing Tarpit" is due to Alan Perlis and refers to the problem of programming minimal machines such as Turing machines, in which "everything is possible, but nothing is easy."

3.1 Tasks as Data Objects

To make the Ada tasking philosophy clearer, let me illustrate its use in defining a type of shared data object.

3.1.1 Example: A request queue

Consider the problem of defining a request queue into which any task can place a request for service (and then continue processing) and from which some other serving task may extract requests for processing. Using traditional semaphores[11], one might generate an implementation with the following general form:

```
Queue: data structure for storing requests;
EntryCounter: SEMA := 0;     -- Requests wait on this semaphore if
                             -- Queue is empty.
Lock: SEMA := 1;             -- Provides mutual exclusion in
                             -- accesses to Queue.
procedure Request(...) is
   begin
      P(Lock);
      place request in Queue;
      V(Lock);
      V(EntryCounter);
   end Request;
procedure Extract(...) is
   begin
      P(EntryCounter);
      P(Lock);
      get next request from Queue;
      V(Lock);
   end Extract;
```

The synchronizing effect desired is that only one task can touch `Queue` at a time and that `Extract` waits until there is something in `Queue`. The semaphores `Lock` and `EntryCounter` provide a mechanism for accomplishing this effect, but do not make it immediately obvious what the desired effect is.

---

[11] I will use the type SEMA to denote the "traditional" counting semaphore. PAda's SEMAPHORE was non-traditional, as discussed in Section 3.2.6.

```
task Queue is
   entry Request(...);
   entry Extract(...);
end Queue;
task body Queue is
   Q: data structure for queue;
begin
   loop
      select
         accept Request(...) do place request in Q end;
      or
         when not Empty(Q) =>
            accept Extract(...) do get next request from Q end;
      end select;
   end loop;
end Queue;
```

Figure 3-1: A simple shared queue in Ada

Using an Ada task, we get a solution such as that shown in Fig. 3-1. Here, the body of `Queue` gives the ordering and the circumstances under which it allows the operations `Request` and `Extract`. It serves, therefore, as a path expression, a concept introduced by Campbell and Habermann [Campbell 74]. The body of `Queue` specifies the intended execution order; Ada provides the mechanism. The function of the semaphore `Lock` is provided by the implied mutual exclusion of entry calls. The function of `EntryCounter` is explicitly provided by the **when** clause, which states precisely the condition the request must wait for—a non-empty queue.

Ada also provides some additional protection for the user beyond that given by "traditional" semaphores. There is no danger of skipping a locking operation, for example. In particular, Ada automatically propagates exceptions in an orderly fashion, undoing locks as it goes.

I believe that the standard Ada programming practice should follow exactly this strategy. Each distinct shared data object should be encapsulated in a task, which will control all access to it. This still leaves to the programmer the task of determining what constitutes a single shared object—another way of saying that the programmer must still choose and state what is the granularity of locking.

3.1.2 A preliminary discussion of implementation strategy

In order to make such a strategy feasible, the language design and implementations will have to concentrate on making the task facility easy to use and efficient to implement. Otherwise, programmers will perforce turn to lower-level mechanisms, and the language will offer them almost no support. It would be unfortunate if Ada tasks were used simply as conventional parallel processes.

No reasonable programmer could be expected to implement request queues in the manner suggested above if it would entail a "full-fledged" task with all the overhead in space and time that this would entail. Fortunately, there is an implementation strategy that avoids any such overhead. Essentially, the semantics of Ada are such that the compiler is (almost) free to implement a task without generating a parallel thread of control specifically for that task.

For example, the body of the task `Queue`, which was specified in Fig. 3-1, might be implemented roughly as shown in Fig. 3-2 (in very pseudo-Ada). The labels `Request_Label` and `Extract_Label` serve as auxiliary entry points in the task body (their use here violates nearly every rule of structured coding, not to mention Ada, but this example is merely supposed to suggest a low-level implementation).

The implementation given here is only intended to be suggestive, and one can, in general, expect that actual code will be better. Habermann and Nassi [Habermann 80] originated the class of techniques shown here. Note that in the presence of multiple accept statements for a given entry, some modification is necessary (there will be several bodies for the entry procedures, which will be accessed through a transfer vector, for example). Note also that almost the same scheme would work if the body of `Queue` were

```
Q: data structure for queue;
procedure Request(...) is
   begin
      Impose mutual exclusion;
      if Request entry not "open"
         then wait (suspending mutual exclusion) until selected;
      end if;
      place request in queue (as in Fig. 3-1);
      Subroutine jump to Request_Label;
   end Request;
procedure Extract(...) is
   begin
      Impose mutual exclusion;
      if Request entry not "open"
         then wait (suspending mutual exclusion) until selected;
      end if;
      get next request from Queue (as in Fig. 3-1);
      Subroutine jump to Extract_Label;
   end Extract;
begin  -- Body of Queue with extended rendezvous removed.

<<Initiate_Label>>  -- Initiation ''calls'' this entry
   loop
      Put Request entry in "open" state;
      if not Empty(Q) then Make Extract entry open end if;
      Select a task at an open entry, if any;
      Return to point of last subroutine jump
         (releasing any mutual exclusion);
     <<Request_Label>>
        -- Anything following do...end would go here
        -- (there is nothing in this example)
      Close all entries;  goto End_Select;
     <<Extract_Label>>
      Close all entries;  goto End_Select;
     <<End_Select>>  null;
     -- Anything following the select statement would go here.
   end loop;
end Queue;
```

Figure 3-2: A low-level implementation for Fig. 3-1.

desired to proceed concurrently outside of rendezvous; the subroutine jumps would be replaced by calls that "wake up" the `Queue` process.

The point is that the `Queue` task need only entail the storage overhead of the queue data structure and a few locks, just as was the case for the "traditional" implementation presented at the beginning of Section 3.1.1. Furthermore, the tasking overhead associated with the entries involves only lock management. In particular, this sort of implementation does not usually require a "cactus stack," because each task that calls `Request` or `Extract` can usually provide all the necessary local storage on its stack[12].

The discussion above was intended to demonstrate the feasibility of using the tasking mechanism of Ada as the exclusive means of managing shared data objects. However, I did qualify the discussion by saying that the compiler is "almost" free to use the strategy outlined. Semantically, the body of `Queue` is supposed to execute in parallel with all its potential callers, whereas the implementation shown in Fig. 3-2 does not have this property. In this case, it does not matter, but we will return to this point in Section 3.5.2.

3.2 Weaknesses in PAda Tasking

For the most part, there are no glaring functional deficiencies in either Ada's or PAda's tasking facility. That is, there are few things that one absolutely cannot do with them and even those exceptions (the inability of one task to suspend another, for example) are easily remedied within individual implementations. Therefore, it is not functionality that I wish to discuss, but rather convenience, safety, and efficiency.

Perhaps "convenience" is not quite the correct word here, as it connotes pandering to programmers' innate laziness. I refer rather to those features of a language that make common program structures easy to conceive, to write, and to understand. Although tasks implement shared data objects, in PAda they were not formulated as data objects. Instead, there was an entire new semantic construct, the task family, which, as we'll see, was merely a reformulation of "data type."

---

[12] The exception is the case of an **accept** within an inner block that declares dynamic data.

3.2.1 Tasks were not types

The discussion of expressiveness in Chapter 1 mentioned the desirability of being able to use a notation that is appropriate for the problem at hand. As we shall see, when dealing with tasks as data objects, it turns out to be natural to want to treat the task specification as a data type—a *template* for objects. This was not directly possible in PAda, and the facilities for doing so indirectly, task families, were quite clumsy when used for that purpose. This section considers the consequences. We will also see that because a programmer could not inform the compiler of his intent to use task families as types, the compiler was forced to produce unnecessarily general code.

A PAda task was a data object, not a data type. Hence the language mechanisms available for constructing types (record types and access types) and for defining operations that take arguments of existing types were not directly available. Thus, if `T` was a (generic) task, one could not directly define a type

```
type Tname is access T;
```

or the like. Likewise, one could not introduce a procedure that would act on any instantiation of `T`, unless that procedure were included in the definition of `T`. As an analogy, imagine the consequences of having to make every routine that took an INTEGER parameter a part of the package defining the type INTEGER. Considering the `Queue` example above, imagine the difficulty of writing a routine `Transfer` that could be given any two `Queues` (i.e., after making the task `Queue` generic) and that would transfer all entries on one to the other. Not even generic procedures would help here; tasks cannot be generic parameters.

As long as tasks were used as processes, in the traditional manner, these objections were not significant. It is when tasks were used as monitors that it became desirable for tasks to look more like ordinary data types.

PAda provided a facility, the *task family*, which allowed a programmer to convert any task into a type, in effect. The indices of the family acted as the names (addresses) of the individual objects (tasks). Hence, they could be used as pointers to the objects and could be embedded in data structures and passed to procedures, just as can values of ordinary types. The technique is similar to that used in FORTRAN to obtain pointers or records (i.e., parallel arrays). Unfortunately, this technique is rather clumsy to use and also causes some efficiency problems that are easily avoided when tasks are treated as ordinary data types.

As a motivating example, consider the problem of defining a database consisting of a large collection of records that are dynamically created and destroyed. The application requires that the records be able to contain references to other records, forming a general graph structure. Finally, the database is to be accessed simultaneously by multiple tasks. Any mutual exclusion is to occur only on individual records and not on the database as a whole (that is, several tasks must be able to access the database concurrently, as long as they operate on distinct records).

The natural thing to do is to make each record a task. This will provide the necessary mutual exclusion. For purposes of this example, let us assume a simple set of operations, namely `Fetch` and `Store`. Further, we'll assume that the data sitting in the various records of the database are all of the single type `Data` (to handle the case of multiple kinds of information, the type `Data` can be a variant record type). In order to get the desired structure, we can use the following package in PAda:

```
package Database is
   type RecordPointer is private;
   Nil: constant RecordPointer;
   type Data is ...  -- The type of data stored in each record.
   function Fetch(x: RecordPointer) return Data;
        -- Fetch data from record referenced by x
   procedure Store(x: RecordPointer; d: Data);
        -- Store d in record referenced by x.
   function Create return RecordPointer;
        -- Return pointer to new record
   procedure Destroy(x: RecordPointer);
        -- Releases storage for record referenced by x.
   MAX_RECORDS: constant INTEGER := 10000;
        -- Maximum number of records that can be
        -- active simultaneously
private
   type RecordPointer is range 0..MAX_RECORDS;
   Nil: constant RecordPointer := 0;
end Database;
```

The package `Database` defines a type, `RecordPointer`, which points to nodes in a database. Each node contains data of type `Data`, which the routines `Fetch` and `Store` can access and modify, given a pointer to the node. The implementation is to impose mutual exclusion on the accesses to the node, so that multiple users can attempt to access a node simultaneously without fear of wreaking havoc with the data it contains.

The body of `Database` represents the class of all database nodes as a task family. To keep track of which elements of the task family are in use at any time, we'll assume the existence of a generic library called `UniqueNamer` which, when instantiated, provides routines for allocating integer tokens in a given range:

```
generic
   Lower, Upper: INTEGER;
package UniqueNamer is
   subtype Token is INTEGER range Lower .. Upper;
   function NewName return Token;
      -- Return an unused integer in Token.
   procedure DeallocateName(x: Token);
      -- Mark x as unused.
end UniqueNamer;
```

The implementation of `UniqueNamer` is left to the reader. With it, we can implement the package `Database` as follows:

```
with UniqueNamer;
package body Database is
   task Records (1..MAX_RECORDS) is
        -- Tasks to hold individual records
      pragma CREATION(DYNAMIC);
      entry Fetch(d: out Data);
      entry Store(d: Data);
   end Records;
   function Fetch(x: RecordPointer) return Data is
      d: Data;
      begin Records(INTEGER(x)).Fetch(d); return d; end;
   procedure Store(x: RecordPointer; d: Data) is
      begin Records(INTEGER(x)).Store(d);  end;
   task Namer is new UniqueNamer(1,MAX_RECORDS);

   function Create return RecordPointer is
         Name: constant INTEGER := Namer.NewName;
      begin
      initiate Records(Name);  return RecordPointer(x);
      end
   procedure Destroy(x: RecordPointer) is
      begin
      abort Records(INTEGER(x));
      Namer.DeallocateName(INTEGER(x));
      end;
   task body Records is
      Z: Data;
   begin
      loop
         select
            accept Fetch(d: out Data) do d := Z; end;
         or
            accept Store(d: Data) do Z := d; end;
         end select
      end loop
   end Records;
end Database;
```

I have encapsulated the data base in a package to insure that only correct `RecordPointers` are used to access the `Records` task. The `CREATION` pragma insures that storage is allocated for records only as they are used. Note the use of the **`abort`** statement in the `Destroy` procedure. This statement is supposed to be used only in emergencies. Unfortunately, it also happens to be the simplest way to insure that that the task to be destroyed will actually be gone when its name is re-used by the `Create` routine. For further discussion of issues surrounding task termination, see Section 3.2.4.

The solution above is quite general and at least some parts of it would be used in any application that required the effect of having pointers to tasks. In fact, I have cut a few corners as it is. For example, I have not insured that `RecordPointers` get initialized properly and have not provided exceptions for the use of the null `RecordPointer`. Also, the library task `UniqueNamer` would have to be provided by the programmer or the installation. It is certainly not a trivial package.

Functionally, this package does a quite satisfactory job of providing, in effect, the type "concurrently accessible record." Programmers can place variables and constants of type `RecordPointer` in the same places they can any ordinary variable. A procedure can take arguments of type `RecordPointer`. Unfortunately, there are still some serious problems of efficiency and convenience.

To start with efficiency, the programmer has little control over the allocation of members of a task family. He can specify dynamic creation and can bound the space allocated, but he does not have any control over the storage allocation scheme used for task data. This is in contrast to the situation for ordinary record types, for which it is possible to write storage allocators in PAda[13]. I see no reason to think that programmers will want any less control over allocation of shared storage than of un-shared storage (especially when I consider the problems involved in programming distributed systems without shared memory). Nor is there any reason, from the point of view of the compiler writer, to prefer to group all instances of a certain class of tasks into what is essentially a single array, any more than there is any motivation to do so with ordinary types of objects.

In fact, the very opposite is true. If the language is effectively going to

---

[13] using the typing loopholes, true, but in an encapsulated package.

require large, dynamically created task families (i.e., created at initiation time), then the compiler has an obligation to manage these families efficiently. For example, a family declared

```
task F(1..1_000_000) is pragma CREATION(DYNAMIC);
```

should require space proportional to the number of members actually initiated. There are tricks that the compiler can use to achieve this effect (hash tables, for example), but in any case it requires some care in the run-time system to do the job properly. Furthermore, a space-efficient implementation is probably going to sacrifice significant time efficiency (e.g., indexing time). While this is probably fine for rare communications among relatively isolated tasks, it is much less desirable when tasks are used as monitors (as elements of task families are apt to be). All this trouble is totally unnecessary if tasks can be treated as are other data objects. The `CREATION` pragma then becomes unnecessary, and task families can be allocated when their declarations are elaborated.

Let's now turn to the problem of programmer convenience. The use (in PAda) of unique integer "names" for tasks, as in the `Database` example, would probably be quite common in practice. As evidence, consider that at least four of the ten solutions submitted by the GREEN team [Honeywell 79] involve some form of this technique[14]. Even when the programmer does not need the full generality of the `Database` solution, he still must go to some trouble to achieve the desired effect. The entire weight of name management rests firmly on the programmer, and, frustratingly, any work the compiler implementor has done to manage access types (essentially the same problem) is unavailable to the programmer. Worse, the `Database` package cannot be made generic in the task `Records` (which would make the whole problem much simpler for the programmer), because packages and tasks are not legal generic parameters.

---

[14] Specifically, solutions 1, 3, 5, and 8.

So far, we have discussed these problems from first principles, in effect. However, the objections raised here are, in fact, instances of failures to satisfy the criteria discussed in Section 1.3. We have been discussing tasks used as data objects. PAda introduced two distinct concepts—the type for ordinary, unshared data objects, and the task family for shared data objects. This was an unnecessary violation of the criterion of simplicity, a failure to exploit the power of the existing type mechanism. Because the task family did not automatically provide the various mechanisms available for types, programmers were necessarily burdened with some of the details of simulating these mechanisms (such as allocation). The task family also suffered from the programmer's inability to express intent; the compiler had to assume that anyone who could mention a task family could reference any member of it at any time. To summarize, the use of task families to fill the role of shared data types complicated the writing of programs, increased the size of the resulting programs, and added to the problems faced by the compiler writer.

3.2.2 Task initiation and allocation

The allocation of a variable is one of the details that conventional von Neumann languages hide from their users. Programmers do not have to be aware of the composition of a variable to be sure that it is properly allocated (and, in Ada, given initial values). However, this hiding of detail extended imperfectly to task objects.

In PAda, the **initiate** statement caused elaboration of the declarations within a task body. Termination (in effect) caused de-allocation of task data. Because of the `CREATION` pragma, some facility of this sort was necessary to indicate when storage was to be allocated. For a couple of reasons, however, explicit initiation of tasks is undesirable.

First, the need for explicit initiation complicates the task of information hiding. As long as a task is declared directly at the current block level, or declared directly within a package body, there is no problem in seeing to it that it gets initiated at the proper time. However, when tasks become parts of data objects, PAda provided no way in which arbitrary initialization code could be invoked when instances of the object were instantiated. This is another example of how PAda interfered with the programmer's desire to free his clients from the details of the implementation of his definition—in this case, from the fact that certain packages required "clean-up" action.

Second, as discussed in Section 3.5.3, the ability to re-initiate causes some subtle complications in the proper handling of aborted tasks.

The PAda Rationale suggested that explicit initiation would make the start-up process more explicit. The primary problem appears to have been that of having a task attempt to rendezvous with another task before the latter had been initiated and was ready to accept entry calls. PAda dictated that in this case, the task attempting the entry call would get an exception. This problem is artificial, however, since nothing prevents the semantics from being that in such situations, the calling task would simply wait.

The Rationale also suggested that **initiate** might be useful in controlled restarts of a crashed system. This is a plausible hypothesis, but the issue is by no means clear. If the "entire world" must be restarted, the best way is probably to abort all tasks and then exit and re-enter some enclosing block. If individual tasks are to be restarted, they will probably have to take some initial actions somewhat different from the usual start-up procedures. That is, they will in general have to be coded to take into account the possibility of being re-started, and the user can be expected to have exercised considerable care. That being the case, we can imagine the following structure in the executable portion of a task:

```
loop
   begin
      body of task
   exception
      when FAILURE => recovery
   end;
end loop;
```

In addition, the user must be careful to supply FAILURE handlers for internal blocks that declare tasks, so that these tasks may be properly aborted. If the FAILURE exception is carefully implemented, it should manage to blast the task out to its exception handlers in most cases. In cases where it cannot, I conjecture that the runtime system may be sufficiently damaged that thoughts of re-initiation are fruitless anyway.

One other place where an explicit initiation operator might be useful is in conjunction with user-defined storage allocation. With the help of the UNCHECKED_CONVERSION function, users can define their own dynamic storage allocators. If the objects to be allocated are tasks—or in general any type of object whose allocation requires some initialization—then some "hook" to the run-time routines that initiate tasks is necessary. It would probably be reasonable, therefore, to introduce another standard generic procedure (called INITIATE, for example).

3.2.3 Subprograms within tasks

In Pada, a subprogram could appear in a task specification. When called by another task, this subprogram would execute in parallel with other activity in the task containing it, and could access any of the local data of the task. If a task had visible subprograms, the compiler could never assume that all calling tasks were finished with its data, with the results that we'll see in this section.

PAda semantics held that declarations in a task body were elaborated after initiation of the task, that initiation could occur any time the task was inactive, and that variables became de-allocated whenever the task terminated. This design decision appears to have had far-reaching consequences on the language design and the efficiency of implementations, almost all of them bad. Basically, all problems stemmed from the fact that variables in the task body, unlike all other variables, could be accessed in statements that could be executing when those variables were not allocated.

Because subprograms within a task could access the task's data directly, PAda had to insure that these subprograms could execute only when the task was active, and that they be aborted if the task containing them was aborted. This requirement had rather grave consequences for the implementation. Apparently, a task T containing a procedure P:

```
task body T is
   procedure P is
      begin body of P end P;
end T;
```

would have to have an implementation something like this:

```
task body T is
   ActiveListLock: SEMA;
   ActiveList: list of tasks that are executing P;
   procedure SignIn(who: task) is
      begin
         P(ActiveListLock);
         Put who on ActiveList;
         V(ActiveListLock);
      end;
   procedure SignOut(who: task) is
      begin
         P(ActiveListLock);
         Take who off ActiveList;
         V(ActiveListLock);
      end;
   procedure P is
      begin
         SignIn(Me);
         body of P;
         SignOut(Me);
      end;
end T;
```

Now when T terminated, whether normally or by aborting, all tasks on `ActiveList` had to first be sent `TASKING_ERROR`.

The point is that there is rather substantial overhead involved in invoking procedures declared within a task, and substantial complexity added to the run-time system. Yet, if the body of P were intended merely to call entries in T in some particular order, with local computation in between, then it would probably suffice simply to raise TASKING_ERROR on the entry calls within P.

These semantics also make TASKING_ERROR into another asynchronous exception (from the point of view of the executing procedures). Section 3.2.5 considers the problems that arise as a result.

Another difficulty, again traceable to the essentially dynamic scoping of task data, crops up in the following example.

```
task body Q is
      -- Large number of declarations;
   A: array (1..n) of NATURAL;
   procedure G is  -- externally visible procedure
      begin
         ...; A(i) := 5; ...
      end G;
end Q;
 ...
initiate Q;  Q.G;
```

The **initiate** statement, by definition, merely begins the elaboration of Q's body. This elaboration (again by definition) includes the elaboration of the declarations of A. There appears to be no guarantee that the variable A will be allocated at the time the call on G accesses it. Note that declarations in a task body are elaborated serially and that their elaboration, in general, can require non-trivial code sequences (to perform initiations, for example). Of course, one could complicate the implementation even more to make all executions of G wait for the declarations to complete. In PAda, however, the result was undefined.

Furthermore, if n in the declaration of A is an imported variable, the storage requirements of Q cannot possibly be determined at scope entry time, no matter how simple Q's statement sequence might be. This absolutely forces heap allocation, which might otherwise be avoided.

The major motivation for the PAda semantics seems to have been a desire to keep the semantics of dynamic creation (especially of members of large task families) consistent with the semantics of task data in general. Section 11.4.4 of the Preliminary Ada Rationale [Ichbiah 79a] mentions other reasons having to do with making start-up order explicit and for giving more control over restarts, but these are not particularly convincing, as discussed in Section 3.2.2.

3.2.4 Termination of tasks

The de-allocation of variables, like their allocation, is another of the details from which von Neumann languages tend to shield their users. Again, this protection, in PAda, did not extend to data objects that were tasks.

Although it is appropriate to wait at block exit for all internally declared active processes to terminate, it is clearly a losing proposition to wait for all SEMAPHOREs to terminate! Most of the GREEN solutions [Honeywell 79] had the interesting property that a program containing one of them would not terminate. The reason, of course, is that each contained a task containing an infinite loop, and the semantics of PAda required that all descendant tasks terminate before the parent does. Many of these solutions would probably be embedded in programs that are not supposed to terminate, but I doubt that this is a universal situation. Any routine or task that forgot to abort or otherwise terminate a single locally declared semaphore would calmly wait at its **end** delimiter forever. This argues for providing a little more help, within the language, for orderly termination of tasks.

Neither the **abort** statement nor raising FAILURE is a preferred way of terminating a task, at least according to the Rationale. There is a good reason for distrusting these two methods—both are asynchronous, and thus make few guarantees about the states in which they leave things. Furthermore, raising FAILURE has the additional problem that should the task being signaled be unprepared to handle the FAILURE exception, it will not be able to terminate any of its internal tasks, and so will "hang". Yet **abort** or FAILURE were the only ways of getting rid of SEMAPHOREs and SIGNALs in PAda.

Again, this problem was a failure to allow the programmer to hide detail—a failure in the abstraction facilities. That is, there was no general way in PAda to completely hide the fact that a package contained a task as part of its implementation[15].

3.2.5 Asynchronous conditions and monitor consistency

We have seen instances of how users of some abstraction may be improperly shielded from details of its implementation. In this section, we have an example of the dual problem: the failure to hide the abstraction from details of its caller. In a sequential language, this presents no serious difficulties; the called procedure has control during its execution. Ada, however, also has parallel constructs, which open various possibilities for interference with an abstraction.

For very good reasons, the Ada philosophy eschews the visible use of asynchronous events. In general, the control flow of a process does not get (logically) interrupted, but accepts requests and notices events at well-defined points (accept statements and the like). This vastly simplifies the problem of understanding and validating the operation of a process. In particular, it simplifies the problem of writing routines to manage data objects (monitors); the language semantics in both Ada and PAda help to guarantee the internal consistency of shared data objects by assuring orderly access of the code

---

[15] It is possible to partially alleviate the problem by establishing the convention that *every* package contain a "finalization" procedure to be called at exit from the block enclosing the package.

that modifies them. The PAda Reference and Rationale both advise caution in the use of the two mechanisms for directly causing asynchronous events: raising FAILURE and executing an **abort**. The Rationale sums this up rather well (section 12.4):

> The ability of one task to raise or to propagate an exception in another task must however be viewed as a possibility with potentially extremely severe consequences.
>
> In no way should such external exceptions be considered as being normal terminating conditions. Interfering asynchronously with the execution of a task may catch it in a state where it is not prepared to respond to such intervention. There is then always a risk of leaving the task in a state of confusion and also, of contaminating other tasks that were communicating with it.

The semantics of PAda led to an unnecessary proliferation of asynchronous events (even in the absence of the "dangerous" explicit modes of termination), making it difficult for tasks to maintain the consistency of their data. Consider the following situation:

```
Task P1:            Task P2:
    P2.F(x)             accept F(x: in out T) do S1; S2;... end;
```

If the rendezvous on the right is in progress at the time that P1 is terminated (via **abort** or by raising FAILURE in P1) the semantics of PAda specified that the rendezvous was to terminate immediately. This was all very well so far as P1 was concerned. It was potentially deadly for P2, however. First, there was the minor annoyance that in order to allow the rendezvous to terminate immediately, PAda disallowed the initiation of any other task during the rendezvous. Secondly, and more seriously, the language made no guarantees whatever about the state of P2's variables at the time the rendezvous was terminated. The best that P2 could do against such a termination was to catch TASKING_ERROR outside of the rendezvous. This all put a rather large burden on P2. One could sometimes use an audit trail, as demonstrated in Section 12.4.7 of the Rationale. However, this technique is rather tedious, to say the least.

The Rationale (Section 12.4.5) claimed that once P1 was asked (forced) to terminate, there would be "no point in pursuing the execution of the **accept** statement since the caller is no longer waiting for its completion." On the contrary, there would be a point: to maintain the consistency of P2's data. In fact, the truth seems to be that there would be no point in terminating the rendezvous. P1's executioner had no quarrel with P2; indeed, he may have needed P2's services. The fact that x would not have to be copied back to P1 is irrelevant.

The semantics of procedures within tasks in PAda introduced another source of logically asynchronous error. Consider the following case in particular:

```
Task P1:                                Task P2:
   procedure G is                          procedure F is ...;
   begin
        ... P2.F;
   end;
```

Suppose that G had been called and had called F. Now suppose that task P1 terminated (normally, even). Not only would G stop execution, F would as well. Furthermore, F would get absolutely no chance whatever to recover and no notification of an error. This is clearly intolerable. Even in the case where F and G were entries, there are still the problems mentioned above; the termination of F was asynchronous so far as P2 was concerned. In addition, F may have initiated or declared tasks. Their disposition when P1 terminated was undefined in PAda.

All of these example of asynchronous events are places where the PAda's semantics failed to hide information properly. One principal idea behind

Ada's tasking and its chief forerunner—Hoare's CSP [Hoare 78]—is that of decomposing a problem in parallelism to several purely sequential problems with small and tightly controlled interaction. The information that is thus hidden is the timing of the various tasks. The problems discussed in this section are instances where the implementation of an abstraction is not protected from details of the context in which it is called (again harking back to the first criterion in section 1.3). In this case, the details were the asynchronous events that might befall its caller.

I suspect that the particular semantics chosen for all the cases we've discussed were motivated by consideration of implementation problems. It may indeed be easier to terminate a task in the obvious way—by summarily popping all rendezvous off its stack and re-awaking the affected tasks with a `TASKING_ERROR` exception—than it is to provide a safer and more helpful implementation. However, here the runtime system is in a far better position than is the programmer to aid in maintaining consistency. It is the obligation of the language designer, therefore, to give all the help he reasonably can in this difficult task.

3.2.6 Signals and semaphores

Ada's built-in generic tasks, `SIGNAL` and `SEMAPHORE`, were totally unnecessary; their purpose was subsumed in (described in terms of, for that matter) the rest of the tasking mechanism. Their inclusion in PAda was a little surprising, considering that the Rationale so convincingly argued against their use (Section 11.4.1). Furthermore, because `SIGNAL`s and `SEMAPHORE`s were both tasks, and not types, they had all the problems discussed in Section 3.2.1. For example, they could not be embedded directly in records.

One justification given for having these tasks was that a compiler could make them special cases and provide a particularly efficient implementation.

However, the techniques of section 3.1.2 will yield very efficient code without any special treatment.

Finally, there is the minor problem that the definition of SEMAPHORE was simply incorrect, or at the very least non-traditional. I am unfamiliar with any other definition of boolean semaphores in which the V operation can block, as they can in the PAda definition:

```
loop
   accept P;  accept V;
end loop;
```

A more traditional definition is as follows.

```
task body SEMAPHORE is
   Open: BOOLEAN := TRUE;
begin
   loop
      select
         when Open =>
            accept P; Open := FALSE;
      or
         accept V;
         select
            accept P; Open := FALSE;
         else
            Open := TRUE;
         end select;
      end select;
   end loop;
end SEMAPHORE;
```

3.2.7 The SELECT statement

In PAda, there were a few blatant failures of expressiveness within the tasking facility—places where a common tasking control structure, while not impossible, was inordinately difficult to write. The most notable was the timed entry call, in which the caller places some limit on the time he is willing to wait for a server to get to him.

In PAda, programs could wait on multiple **accept** or **delay** statements (using the **select** statement), but not on multiple calls on entries. There seem to be no methodological reasons for this limitation on the **select** statement, although there are some issues of implementation.

Several classes of example indicated a need for an extension to the **select** statement. A task might want to time-out on an entry call, or it might want to make an entry call only if it would not block. Sometimes, reformulating a program so that an entry call became an **accept** would work, but this generally resulted in obscurity and was usually impractical.

There was a partial solution—introducing auxiliary tasks. For example, the procedure `Timed_A1` below calls the entry `P.A` and times out after one second.

```
procedure Timed_A1 is
   task Wait is
      entry A_Done;
   end Wait;
   task DoA;
   task body Wait is
   begin
      select
         accept A_Done;
      or
         delay 1.0 * SECONDS;
      end select;
      abort DoA;
   end Wait;
   task body DoA is
   begin
      P.A;  Wait.A_Done;
   end DoA;
begin
   initiate DoA,Wait;
end Timed_A1;
```

The solution above is not particularly perspicuous; it is not particularly safe (note the race condition); and it is not particularly efficient. There is nothing to be gained by simplifying and shrinking a run-time system if one result is a large number of programs such as that above. Most programmers would find it much more natural to write

```
procedure Timed_A2 is
   begin
      select
         P.A;
      or
         delay 1.0 * SECONDS;
      end select;
   end Timed_A2;
```

These objections are instances of a general lack of expressiveness—a failure to completely provide notation that is natural to the problem area. Here, the PAda **select** statement—the single mechanism provided for awaiting one of several possible events—did not cover at least one fairly common case of multiple event (i.e., where one event is a call and the other a time-out). Furthermore, there was no definitional capability that would allow us to easily extend the class of "awaitable" event, to encapsulate the construction that produced `Timed_A1`, above.

3.3 Revisions of Preliminary Ada's Tasking

As a result of the preceding analysis, I was able to convince the Ada design team to make several changes to PAda's tasking facility to produce the facility found in Revised Ada.

1. Task specifications became type specifications. Individual task objects became variables of these types. The existing mechanisms for creating structured types made task families redundant, and they were eliminated.

2. Task initiation became automatic upon creation of a task object, just as variable initialization is automatic upon allocation of the variable.

3. Subprograms within task specifications were outlawed.

4. A restricted kind of standard entry—**terminate**—was added to allow a task object to sense that its enclosing context is quiescent and to exit when this happens.

5. The semantics of **abort** and `FAILURE` were changed so that they now affect only the task being aborted or signaled, and not necessarily another task called by the affected task. Furthermore,

subprograms exported by tasks—another source of asynchronous interrupts—were eliminated.

6. The generic tasks `SEMAPHORE` and `SIGNAL` were removed.

7. Entry calls were extended to allow a limited form of **select**, in which a single entry could appear together with a **delay** or **else** clause. This provided a facility for performing time-outs on entry calls.

Points 1, 2, 3, and 6 are fairly direct responses to the analysis in the preceding section. The third (disallowing subprograms within the visible parts of tasks, as discussed in section 3.2.3) was a simple method of relieving the compiler's lack of information about who might be executing one of these procedures. An alternative would have been to allow such subprograms to be called even if the task itself had been terminated; then the compiler would not have to make any assumptions, since it would never have to terminate the execution of one of these visible subprograms.

The fourth revision (**terminate**) allows tasks used as variables to be de-allocated like variables, thus hiding details of the implementation of these variables—namely, their "taskness." The fifth revision also facilitates freedom from detail, this time on the part of the called task, which is no longer interrupted during rendezvous by events that occur asynchronously to its caller.

The last point, I must confess, is a fairly *ad hoc* solution to the perceived problem—an additional piece of semantic stew rather than a general definitional mechanism for defining events. Another, more definitional, approach was that taken in the RED language [Nestor 79], in which the equivalent of **select** (called WAIT) was actually a generic control structure that could be parameterized, in effect, by user-definable events. Although I consider an approach like RED's preferable, it is still the case that the known implementation schemes for the **select** with the restricted set of events allowed in Ada are more efficient than those for RED's more general scheme.

More precise semantic details of the changes listed above are in the revised Reference Manual [Honeywell 80] (which we will call the RRM hereafter). The rest of this section is devoted to examples and certain consequences of the revised design.

3.3.1 Exceptions in the caller during rendezvous

The decision in Revised Ada to make rendezvous oblivious to abnormal termination of the caller was motivated by the consistency arguments of Section 3.2.5. To see the implications, consider again the case

```
Task P1:          Task P2:
    P2.F(x)           accept F(x: in out T) do S1; S2;... end;
```

The run-time system delays the receipt of a FAILURE exception by P1 until the rendezvous finishes (assuming one was in progress at the time of receipt). The task P2 never sees any sign that P1 has been zapped, any more than it would see any sign that another task had enqueued on an entry of P1 during the rendezvous. In short, every task minds its own business. The PAda definition already said (Reference Section 11.5) that FAILURE "supersedes all other exceptions not yet handled or received before FAILURE is handled," so there is no problem of multiple exceptions resulting from the call on P2.F.

If P1 is terminated, the only difference is that the rendezvous (in effect) will return to a dead task, presumably causing an immediate call of the runtime system. Note that the semantics of rendezvous are such that as long as all parameters are copied, it is irrelevant what happens to P1's data.

As long as there is no need for expeditious termination of rendezvous, the restriction (Reference Manual section 9.5) that the bodies of **accept** statements may not initiate tasks is no longer necessary. Elimination of this restriction also simplified separate compilation, oddly enough. A separately compiled procedure that is called from the body of an **accept** statement could not initiate a task in PAda. Unfortunately, the specifications of this procedure (i.e., that portion which must appear in the calling task) do not contain sufficient information to check statically that this restriction is observed[16].

3.3.2 The clean-up issue

There are usually two sides to any design decision, and the case of the revised handling of **abort** and FAILURE is no exception. The semantics of Revised Ada insure that a task being called does not get interrupted asynchronously if its caller is destroyed. A consequence of this, however, is that the called task does not get notified of the dire fate of its caller. Suppose that the called task is some sort of resource manager and has an entry called, say, `AllocateResource`. If a caller of `AllocateResource` gets aborted during execution of the rendezvous, one could argue that it would be useful for the resource manager to take note of this fact and undo the allocation. This is the effect of the following PAda schema:

```
task ResourceManager is
   entry AllocateResource(...);
    . . .
end ResourceManager;
```

[16]A similar difficulty arose with procedures called from within functions, which could not modify global variables or allocate any variables dynamically. This is one of several reasons why various reviewers suggested that the semantics of functions be loosened, and that the revised language did so.

```
task body ResourceManager is
   . . .
begin
   . . .
   begin -- Inner block for catching exception
      Record the allocation state;
      accept AllocateResource(. . .)
         do Perform allocation; end;
   exception
      when TASKING_ERROR =>
         Restore stored allocation state;
   end;  -- Inner block
   . . .
end ResourceManager;
```

However, having gone to this trouble, we do not really have a very general solution. It is only a matter of timing whether the forcible termination of the calling task takes place *during* or *just after* the rendezvous with `AllocateResource`. We'd like the same restorative action in *both* cases, but only in the former case—when the termination happens to occur during the rendezvous—will it actually take place.

To formulate this problem more generally, what we have is some resource manager, say R, which services or interacts with a set of clients, $\{C_i\}$. Each client engages in some protocol of transactions with R, such as

```
Request facility A from R;
Return facility A to R;
```

If one of the C_i gets abnormally interrupted, R ought to be notified to tell it that this client will no longer communicate. Seen in this way, it should be clear that the PAda exception-handling mechanism was at far too low a level to be useful in handling this problem (so, for that matter, is the mechanism in Revised Ada).

In general, therefore, the act of shutting down an Ada task prematurely is a high-level abstraction. Such language features as **abort** and the tasking exceptions are most properly seen as low-level tools with which to *implement* instances of this abstraction. It would be possible to design higher-level tools into Ada, for example something along the lines of the exception mechanisms that Levin studied [Levin 77]. However, there are also ways to use the mechanisms of Ada as it stands to this end.

As a concrete example, suppose that the resource manager R has the following form.

```
task R is
   entry Assign(x: out TapeDrive);
   entry Release(x: TapeDrive);
end R;
```

and that the clients, C_i are supposed to eventually call Release for each drive that they get via Assign. Suppose (to start with) that each C_i has a form something like this:

```
task body Ci is
   . . .
   Resources: ListOfTapeDrives;
   . . .
begin
   -- Body of Ci.  Adds TapeDrives to Resources as they
   -- are acquired from R and removes them as they are Released.
end Ci;
```

Before aborting C_i, we would like to release all its TapeDrives. One way is to use the command

```
raise Ci'FAILURE;
```

which raises the exception FAILURE in C_i (asynchronously) rather than simply aborting it, and to add an appropriate exception handler to the body of C_i:

```
task body Ci is
   . . .
begin
   . . .
exception
   when FAILURE =>
      For each item, x, in Resources, R.Release(x);
end Ci;
```

Now this solution solves the clean-up problem, but has some difficulties. First, it requires that the C_i maintain the information of what to clean up and how. That is, we have not encapsulated the operation "clean up my account with R," which is probably useful for all of R's clients. Secondly, in the solution above, the operations needed to keep track of what resources C_i owns are not encapsulated with the calls on R to obtain and release resources. Therefore, the programmer will have to be careful that an attempt to raise FAILURE on C_i at an inopportune moment (i.e., just before it is recorded in Resources) does not cause C_i to lose track of the last resource allocated.

To meet these objections, we can reformulate R so that it reflects the notion that it has clients, as well as individual requests. For example, we could use the following package specification for R:

```
package R is
   generic package Liaison is   -- instantiated for each client.
      procedure Assign(x: out TapeDrive);
      procedure Release(x: TapeDrive);
      procedure CleanUp;
   end Liaison;
end R;
```

A client now hooks into R like this:

```
task body Ci is
   package MyLiaison is new R.Liaison;
   . . .
begin
   -- Body of Ci.  Uses MyLiaison.Assign and
   -- MyLiaison.Release to obtain and return resources from R.
exception
   when FAILURE => MyLiaison.CleanUp;
end Ci;
```

All data on how to clean up is now encapsulated in the module R, which is in a convenient position to insure the appropriate indivisibility of operations that maintain the record of resources used by each client.

Figure 3-3 shows a possible body for R. The internal task R.Manager does the actual work of keeping track of who has used what. I have not included its body in the figure, since the details are not particularly important. Each instance of R.Liaison "checks in" with R.Manager to receive an identification (Me), which it uses to identify itself in subsequent calls. The resulting solution is still not perfect—for example, the CleanUp operation is

```
package body R is
   subtype ClientId is INTEGER range 0 .. INTEGER'LAST;

   task Manager is
      entry GetId(x: out ClientId);
         -- Hand out a unique integer to be used to identify an
         -- instance of Liaison.
      entry Assign(Who: ClientId; x: out TapeDrive);
         -- Return assigned device and record requester.
      entry Release(x: TapeDrive);
      entry ReleaseAll(Who: ClientId);
         -- Release all devices currently owned by Who.
   end Manager;

   package body Liaison is
      Me: ClientId;        -- Unique ID of this instantiation.
      procedure Assign(x: out TapeDrive) is
         begin  Manager.Assign(Me,x);  end;

      procedure Release(x: TapeDrive) is
         begin  Manager.Release(x);  end;

      procedure CleanUp is
         begin  Manager.ReleaseAll(Me);  end;

   begin
      Manager.GetId(Me);
   end Liaison;

   task body Manager is
      . . .
   end Manager;
end R;
```

Figure 3-3: Revised body of R.

not invoked automatically—but is a feasible way to, in effect, implement a more general scheme for broadcasting exceptions than Ada provides.

In the solution above, the task that takes it upon itself to forcibly terminate one of the C_i does so by raising FAILURE for that client in order to induce it to clean up and go away. In fact, it is possible to *implement* the raising of FAILURE (in effect), with judicious use of **abort**. Thus, an alternative to the scheme outlined to this point is to surround each client with a package, as in Fig. 3-4. Here, **abort** is used as the primitive operation that implements the

```
package Pi is
   task Ci is . . . end Ci;
   procedure Kill;
end Ci;

package body Pi is

   package MyLiaison is new R.Liaison;

   task body Ci is
      . . .
   begin . . . end Ci;

   procedure Kill is
      begin
         abort Ci;  MyLiaison.CleanUp;
      end Kill;
end Pi;
```

Figure 3-4: Using **abort** to implement **raise** FAILURE.

"high-level" abnormal-termination operator, Kill[17].

In summary, we have seen that the original way of propagating **aborts** and FAILURE exceptions in PAda was an inadequate way to deal with the real problem of cleaning up after a task that makes use of shared facilities. Furthermore, we have seen an approach to solving this problem in Revised Ada.

3.4 Examples

This section presents two sample programs written in Revised Ada. The first is a re-working of the Database example in Section 3.2.1. The second illustrates the use of timed entry calls and further illustrates the utility of tasks as data objects. In both cases, we will see major reductions in the difficulty of coding. I urge the reader to attempt writing the second example in PAda as a comparison.

---

[17] Indeed, the 1982 revision of Ada actually eliminates the FAILURE exception altogether, in part because of arguments like this.

3.4.1 Database, revisited

Figure 3-5 shows the specification and body of a package that provides the services of the Database package in Section 3.2.1. Because RecordPointers are now ordinary access (pointer) variables, the system-provided functions for allocating dynamic storage now apply, without the programmer having to re-create them.

```
package Database is
   type Rec;
   type RecordPointer is access Rec;
        -- Create is now done with new.
        -- Destroy is done automatically by the system, or
        -- by the pre-defined explicit FREE routine.
   type Data is ...  -- Type of data stored in each record.
   task type RecordPack is
      entry Fetch(d: out Data);
        -- Return data in record in d.
      entry Store(d: Data);
        -- Store d in record.
   end RecordPack;
end Database;

package body Database is
   task body Record is
      Z: Data;
   begin
      loop
         select
            accept Fetch(d: out Data) do d := Z end;
         or
            accept Store(d: Data) do Z := d end;
         end select;
      end loop;
   end Record;
end Database;
```

Figure 3-5: Revised Database example.

3.4.2 An asynchronous server

Suppose that tasks are to submit requests for computations to a single server task. Upon making a request, a task is to be released immediately and is to be able to return later to retrieve the results of computation. In retrieving results, tasks are to specify the maximum time they will wait, after which they will be released and be free to pick up the results later. To simplify matters, assume that the data operated upon consist of a single object of type T and that the procedure G performs the desired computation.

In the solution to follow, I have minimized the number of tasks in order to demonstrate the use of monitor packages and to show how the programmer can state clearly what he intends in the way of physical parallelism. In this solution, the compiler will not have to introduce any process context overheads (either space or time). A similar solution in PAda introduces a large number of tasks, some of which require process contexts, but most of which don't.

First, it is useful to define a datatype Box, similar to the MAILBOX type in RED (Nestor [Nestor 79]). Figure 3-6 contains the definition. This definition, of course, has considerable utility outside of the current application.

Figure 3-7 shows a program that uses mailboxes twice, once for the serving process' queue, and once to define a "basket" for returning results. There is no practical need to provide a time-out facility in this package, as a user can write it himself with rather little writing, and possibly some gain in readability.

Here is an example of how a task might use the package:

```
use Server;
MyBox: RSVP := new RSVP;
begin
   ...
   Request(Q,MyBox);
   ...
   select
      MyBox.Receive(Answer);
   or
      delay 0.01 * SECONDS;
   end select;
   ...
```

```
generic
   type Q is private;
   SIZE: NATURAL;
package Boxes is
   task type Box is -- A FIFO queue containing up to SIZE items
                    -- of type Q.
      entry Send(x: Q);
         -- Place x into queue, waiting until not full first.
      entry Receive(x: out Q);
         -- Take next Q out of queue, waiting if empty.
   end Box;
end Boxes;

package body Boxes is
   task body Box is
      n: range 0 .. SIZE := 0;
      Slots: array (1 .. SIZE) of Q;
   begin
   loop
      select
         when (n<SIZE) and (CLOSE'COUNT=0) =>
            accept Send(x: Q) do n := n+1;  Slots(n) := x; end;
      or when n>0 =>
             accept Receive(x: out Q)
                do x := Slots(n); n := n-1; end;
      or terminate;
      end select;
   end loop;
   end Box;
end Boxes;
```

Figure 3-6: A generic mailbox (FIFO queue).

3.5 Implementation Considerations

For Ada's tasking model to be successful, the various implementation details from which it relieves the programmer must not come back to haunt him in the form of miserable performance. In this section, we consider the a few of the implementation issues raised by the tasking mechanism.

3.5.1 Production-quality code for monitors, with some help

Section 3.1.2 sketched an implementation strategy that allowed a compiler to implement monitor tasks without actually creating a new executable context, and hence without incurring the overheads required for general, concurrently executable tasks (for brevity, I shall call these latter "processes"

```
package Server is
   package Basket is new Boxes(T,1);
   type RSVP is access Basket.Box;
   procedure Request(x: T; Result: RSVP);
        -- Request that x be computed and returned in Result
        -- Raises Full if too many pending requests.
   exception Full;
end Server;
package body Server is
   Max_Requests: constant INTEGER := 100;
   type Item is
      record
         Val: T;
         Result: RSVP;
      end record;
   package Queue is new Boxes(Item,Max_Requests);
   task Processor;
   task body Processor is
   Next: Item;
   begin
      loop
         Queue.Receive(Next);
         G(Next.Val);
         select
            Next.Result.Send(Next.Val);
         else  --If this entry call blocks, something is wrong,
               --so give up and service other users.
            null;
         end select;
      end loop;
   end Processor;
   procedure Request(x: T; Result: RSVP) is
      begin
         select
            Queue.Send(Item(x,Result));
         else raise Full;
         end select;
      end Request;
end Server;
```

Figure 3-7: Example of a "come back later" server.

from now on[18]). Of course, the technique is not generally applicable. For example, consider the following Ada fragments:

```
In task P1:                          In task P2:
   accept E1 do S1 end;                 P1.E1;
   P2.G;  -- Any entry in P2.           S2;
```

[18] I am aware that the terminology can be confusing. The GREEN team used the term "processor" here, but some readers (and the author) may confuse this with a piece of hardware.

Although the compiler may always arrange for the elaboration of the extended rendezvous (`S1`) within task `P2`'s context, it cannot always count on being able to execute the rest of `P1` in that context (up to the next **`accept`** or **`select`**), as was done in section 3.1.2. In the case above, particularly, it would be disastrous for `P2` to attempt to elaborate the entry call `P2.G` in the ordinary way; it would block waiting for itself.

Of course, a compiler cannot decide, in general, whether to set up a separate physical process for a task. On the one hand, even if there are no entry calls or **`delay`** statements within the body of a task (outside of its **`accept`** statements), one might still want to execute statements outside of **`accept`** statements concurrently with other tasks. On the other hand, even if there are entry calls within a task, there are circumstances under which it would still be legitimate not to create a process. One circumstance is that the programmer knows that no deadlock will occur and that he does not care about priority scheduling. A compiler could not detect this situation in general without hints from the programmer. This suggests that implementations will want to install pragmas[19] communicating such things as the fact that a task will never block or loop outside a rendezvous.

At the same time, there is a large class of interesting programs for which a compiler might well determine automatically that no separate process context is necessary. This class includes those programs that contain nothing outside **`accept`** statements (except pre-defined operations on the built-in types) and in which all loops outside **`accept`** statements are broken by **`accept`** statements (or **`select`** statements that contain only **`accept`** statements.)

---

[19] In Ada, a *pragma* is a message to the compiler.

3.5.2 Production quality code for monitors, automatically

The purpose of a production quality (or "optimizing") compiler is to relieve the programmer of the burdens of figuring out the "right" (smallest, most efficient) low-level coding or representation for his program. In the case of programs involving tasks, one of these burdens is that of deciding on a mechanism for mutual exclusion. In this section, we briefly consider some possible ways that a compiler can represent some Ada tasks.

Consider the following task

```
task ProtectedVariable is
   entry Get(d: out T);
   entry Put(d: T);
end ProtectedVariable;
task body ProtectedVariable is
   x: T;
begin
   loop
      select
         accept Get(d: out T) do  d := x;  end;
      or
         accept Put(d: T) do  x := d;  end;
      end select;
   end loop;
end ProtectedVariable;
```

Section 3.1.2 sketched one possible implementation. Another way of viewing what a compiler might do here is

```
task body ProtectedVariable is
   x: T;
   type Names is (GetName, PutName);
   Q: array (Names) of queue_of_tasks;
   procedure Get(d: out T) is
      begin
         Prolog(GetName);  d := x;  Epilog;
      end;
   procedure Put(d: T) is
      begin
         Prolog(PutName);  x := d;  Epilog;
      end;
```

The `Prolog` and `Epilog` procedures are essentially as described by Nassi and Habermann [Habermann 80]:

```
procedure Prolog(n: Names) is
   begin
      if monitor is being used or n not open
         then enqueue current task on Q[n]; suspend self;
      end if;
   end;
procedure Epilog is
   begin
      compute up to next accept or select and determine a
         new set of open entries.
      if for some open entry n, Q[n] is not empty
         then release a process on Q[n];
      end if;
   end;
```

When not suspended, these operations must proceed indivisibly, of course.

Note that in this case, as some simple flow analysis will indicate, there is only one possible set of open entries (i.e., the set of all entries). Therefore, `Prolog` and `Epilog` simplify to

```
procedure Prolog(n: Names) is
   begin
      if monitor being used
         then enqueue current task on Q[n]; suspend self;
      end if;
   end;
procedure Epilog is
   begin
      if for some open entry named n, Q[n] is not empty
         then release a process on Q[n];
      end if;
   end;
```

The semantics of select (specifically, the non-deterministic[20] selection of entries) now allow the task queues to be merged, giving

[20]The PAda Reference used the term "random" and the Rationale suggested the use of true statistical randomness to prevent programmers from making assumptions. This was highly undesirable. The implementation here, for example, provides an example where introducing a random number generator would really foul things up. The point should have been that the runtime system is not restricted in its choice of implementation. This correction appears in the revised manual.

```
procedure Prolog(n: Names)  is
   begin
      if monitor being used
         then enqueue current task on Q;  suspend self;
      end if;
   end;
procedure Epilog is
   begin
      if Q is non-empty
         then release a process on Q;
      end if;
   end;
```

But these are just the standard boolean P and V operations.

To go one step further, suppose that assignment and fetching of T are indivisible operations (a fact which presumably a compiler would know). Then the two competing critical regions within Get and Put may be executed without any locking, and ProtectedVariable can be represented as a single T. Note that this optimization is possible only if both regions are effectively indivisible[21]. It is desirable to let the compiler make the decision of whether to perform the lock-removal optimization, especially if portability is an issue.

3.5.3 Maintaining consistency of monitors

One of the problems with having passive shared data objects (here, monitors) is that a process operating on one of them may get itself abnormally terminated, with grave consequences to the monitor and thus to other processes using the monitor. The runtime system, therefore, must be careful to try to keep monitors "running". That is, although a compiler may use the calling processes to run the code of a monitor, it must maintain the semantics that logically, the monitor is itself a process.

---

[21] A region is effectively indivisible as long as it contains only one indivisible access to shared data. Extra computation involving local data (such as array index computations) does not matter.

To be a little more explicit, let us suppose that the underlying operating system has some notion of a concurrently executable entity, which I'll call a p-task (for physical task). The run-time may use a p-task to implement a task (process). Then, when the process invokes a monitor, the semantics allows the run-time to use the same p-task to execute the monitor's code. If now the process is terminated, the p-task should not be terminated, but should continue executing the monitor. When this finishes (comes to an accept, e.g.) the p-task will try to go back to executing the process, but will find (through a flag, say) that the process no longer exists, and will take appropriate action (perhaps destroying itself). The same applies to the `FAILURE` exception, since the proposed semantics allows execution of monitors to take precedence over execution of tasks.

Of course, it would be nice if we could guarantee that monitors would continue running even if p-tasks got destroyed. However, inasmuch as this may very well mean requiring the run-time system to pick up after a processor that gets shot to pieces, it is probably too much to expect in general.

3.6 Summary

In this chapter, we saw several principles at work. First, the PAda task family was an example of both unnecessary complexity—a new concept added to the language that could have been explained using the existing type mechanism—, of lack of expressiveness, and of lack of expressiveness of intent—the array of task formulation gives the compiler less information than it could use about the lifetime of tasks. Second, explicit initiation and termination, as well as the asynchronous interruption of servers, were examples of how PAda made it difficult to encapsulate detail.

Chapter 4
Design Alternatives in Ada

The preceding two chapters have dealt with problems in Preliminary Ada that have been corrected (or materially alleviated) in Revised Ada. These problems consisted mostly of violations of the various criteria given in section 1.3. In the process, we saw a few examples of why these criteria are reasonable. For example, in section 3.2.1, we saw an example of a particularly clumsy program that became quite manageable when tasks were given the full definitional generality (expressiveness) of types. In section 2.2.3, we saw how the inability of a compiler to assume certain information (the programmer's inability to express intent), could cause problems that were easily fixed by (in that case) eliminating unnecessary generality.

In this chapter, we consider design alternatives in Revised Ada, and in the process, further validate the criteria by showing how attention to and use of definitional expressiveness, in particular, can simplify a language. Each section considers the design of some piece of the Ada language and develops an alternative design that improves on the original in one or more of the following ways:

- Simplifying the Ada language proper by removing some built-in facility and recasting it within the existing abstraction mechanisms;

- Augmenting the abstraction mechanisms with some relatively simple facilities that in turn permit simplification as above;

- Recasting some cluster of abstraction mechanisms into some simpler and more general mechanisms.

Again, a large portion of language evaluation is taste. The sorts of changes detailed above will lead to different solutions to certain programming problems. Some readers, for reasons of taste or custom, are bound to find these new solutions less satisfactory than the originals. In evaluating these alternative designs, therefore, we must compare what is lost with what is gained—in expressiveness, documentation, freedom from detail, performance, and simplicity—and must set some priorities on these criteria to eliminate that which is merely subjective. In particular, modifications affecting only syntactic or lexical details are less important than those affecting what information can be encapsulated.

My purpose here is not simply to propose a revision of the Ada language, but more importantly to demonstrate how modest improvements of abstraction facilities can lead both to a substantial increase in expressive power and a smaller language. Furthermore, we need not pay for these improvements with unacceptable run-time overheads.

In a sense, this chapter is a continuation of research that began with the Tartan language [Shaw 78]. Tartan was a response to what we (its authors) saw as the unnecessary complexity of the four designs that had been proposed (in early 1978) for the DOD-1 language (which was to become Ada). We attempted to make Tartan's abstraction mechanisms powerful enough to render it unnecessary to wire in many of the facilities that various parts of Ada's future clientele had requested. In this, I believe, we mostly succeeded. However, the language was a sketch—indeed was never intended to be any more than that.

One might, therefore, criticize the approach taken in this chapter, arguing that I could present a cleaner result by completing the Tartan design rather than attempting to incrementally re-design an existing language. Indeed, existing parts of Ada will definitely get in our way in the sections to follow. My purpose, however, is to give some reason to think that the final design is not a radical departure from the type of language design that has already been judged acceptable.

4.1 Derived types

The derived type facility in Ada is a mechanism for defining new types that "inherit" their representation and some of their operations from previously-defined types. In this section, I shall attempt to show that the mechanism is superfluous—an unnecessary complication of the language.

Section 4.1.1 will review the derived type mechanism as it currently stands in Ada. Section 4.1.2 will then argue that other facilities of Ada adequately provide the functionality of derived types. This section, in other words, is an application of the criterion of simplicity discussed in section 1.3—of getting maximum mileage out of a language's abstraction facilities.

4.1.1 Review of derived types in current Ada

Besides the standard Pascal-like type constructors for array, record, and pointer types, Ada provides a mechanism for creating a new type out of an existing type. The declaration

```
type T2 is new T1;
```

declares T2 to designate a type distinct from all others, but having many of the same characteristics as T1. Specifically, **T2** has the same domain, aggregates, literals, attributes, representation (usually), default values, and component selectors as T1. Values of the two types T1 and T2 may be inter-converted using built-in transfer functions T1 (converts to type T1 from type T2) and T2.

For each subprogram that involves arguments or results of type T1 and that is defined in the same package specification as T1, a similar subprogram is defined for type T2. This "derived" subprogram has a specification in which T2 is uniformly substituted for T1 and a body that performs appropriate coercions and invokes the original subprogram. The pre-defined types—INTEGER, FLOAT, etc.—and the standard arithmetic operators on them, are assumed to have been declared in the package STANDARD for purposes of this definition.

Certain features of the language are defined in terms of derived types. The declaration

```
type INT is range L .. U;
```

is defined to be identical to

```
type INT$ is new INTEGER_TYPE$;
subtype INT is INT$ range L .. U;
```

where INT$ is a unique compiler-generated name and INTEGER_TYPE$ is one of the built-in integer types (INTEGER, LONG_INTEGER, etc.), selected by the compiler to contain the specified range of values. Since the compiler makes this choice, the programmer does not need to change his program text when moving it to a machine with a different word size.

4.1.2 Removing derived types

One rather common comment about the derived type mechanism defined in the preceding section is that it is rather complex. The summary given there was informal and incomplete, but even explanations at that level seem to leave beginning Ada programmers (and implementors, for that matter) in confusion. The complexity is enough to outweigh any minor advantages it might afford, and so we must see if there are *substantial* reasons for its existence.

The Ada Language Design Team has listed four motivations for the derived type facility [Ada 80][22]:

- "Hierarchical type composition [as in] Simula: [the ability to add] functional attributes at each derivation level."

- " 'Poor man's strong typing':

```
type WEIGHT is new INTEGER;
type LENGTH is new INTEGER;
   -- [cannot] mix weights and lengths ''
```

- Change of representation: if derived type T2 is explicitly given a representation specification (indicating the offsets and widths of record fields and other low-level details), then conversion between T2 and its parent type also effects a change of representation.

- "For construction of private types. Derived types provide an unambiguous way of denoting the operations of the representation type and of the private type."

To provide a basis of comparison, let's take the somewhat drastic step of deleting derived types altogether and then examine the consequences in light of each of the motivations just listed. To do the deletion, we must first make some provision for integer and floating-point types, since—as mentioned in the preceding section—their semantics is defined using derived types. The most obvious course is to simply limit these types to those provided in the package STANDARD. That is, we shrink the syntax of type_definition (RRM, section 3.3) to

---

[22]Two other motivations given in that document have been rendered obsolete by revisions.

```
type_definition ::=
    enumeration_type_definition | fixed_type_definition
  | array_type_definition       | record_type_definition
  | access_type_definition      | private_type_definition

fixed_type_definition ::= fixed_point_constraint
```

by eliminating the two forms

```
type INT is range L .. U;
type REAL is digits D ...;
```

Having done so, we now turn to the consequences

4.1.2.1 Numeric representation selection

The automatic selection of numeric representation in Ada is an attempt to overcome the maintenance problems associated with changing the ranges or precisions of numeric variables. In FORTRAN, such a change requires replacing one type identifier with another in a potentially large and distributed set of declarations. In Pascal, there is but one integer and floating-point type. One could use Pascal's subrange types to hide the existence of several underlying hardware representations for the various precisions, but this runs into a slight implementation problem with the necessary precision of intermediate results[23].

At first glance, one might think that the elimination of the automatic integer and floating type selection features would force programmers to start using the pre-defined types `INTEGER`, `FLOAT`, etc., directly. This, in turn, would mean that a programmer who wished to move his program from, say, a machine with a 32-bit word size to one with a 16-bit word size would be forced

---

[23] All real arithmetic, for example, would be done with the maximum precision. In general, integer arithmetic would have to be done using the maximum-sized representation for intermediate values, although the compiler could, at least in some cases, determine that a smaller representation would suffice by looking at the declared ranges.

to change all instances of INTEGER in his program to LONG_INTEGER. In other words, it appears that the elimination of automatic selection of numeric representations leads to problems with portability and maintenance.

However, there is a simple alternative. Rather than declaring

```
type INT is L .. U;
```

we can instead declare

```
subtype INT is INTEGER_TYPE$ range L .. U;
```

where *we* select INTEGER_TYPE$ to have the necessary range. The compiler will check the adequacy of the type we choose; it is an error for L or U to fall outside the domain of INTEGER_TYPE$. Now the problem of porting to a new machine of expanding the representation to deal with an expanded application only involves changing a few subtype declarations. Likewise, instead of

```
type REAL is digits 10;
```

we write

```
subtype REAL is LONG_FLOAT digits 10;
```

Again, the compiler will check that LONG_FLOAT will accommodate ten decimal digits of precision. The compiler does not check to see if the programmer has been over-generous with the representation (e.g., using LONG_FLOAT where FLOAT would suffice), but this is hardly a serious problem.

In effect, we are using subtype definitions to abstract away from our machine's word size. The purpose of automatic selection of numeric representation is to make this completely automatic. What we've seen here is a technique that automates most of the procedure of adapting one's program to a new word size and checking that the representations chosen are adequate. All that is left to the programmer is to change a few lines for each new machine to which he ports his program. (There is one other significant semantic difference: The names introduced by subtype declarations are not distinct types. This is a separate issue, however, and we'll come back to it in Section 4.1.2.3).

The practice of using subtype declarations such as those above avoids an annoyance that crops up with mathematical software. The basic problem is that in order to write a mathematical package that operates on, say, floating point numbers, one must first have one or more floating point types with which to specify and write the package. The solution currently advocated by at least part of the Language Design Team is to make packages such as MATH_FUNCTIONS be generic in the type REAL. The package using MATH_FUNCTIONS then defines the type REAL and the communication problem goes away. Rather, it goes away until the client package *itself* becomes a library package, at which point it, too, must be made generic the type REAL. This solution appears workable, but the necessity of all the explicit generic instantiations is apt to be annoying, especially if one's compiler is naive about collapsing together the resulting identical object code modules.

Another solution is to have the package's author write

```
package MATH_FUNCTIONS is
    type REAL is digits PRECISION;
    function SIN(x: REAL) return REAL;
        . . .
end MATH_FUNCTIONS;
```

but then the users of MATH_FUNCTIONS must use (or coerce to) the type MATH_FUNCTIONS.REAL. If a user requires more than one of these independently-compiled library packages, he has a slight communication problem on his hands; results coming from one package must be converted before being fed to another.

In contrast to these two approaches, using subtypes of the pre-defined types works quite smoothly. There is manifestly no communication problem and no need for generic instantiations. By overloading the package's routines for each built-in numeric type:

```
package MATH_FUNCTIONS is
    function SIN(X: FLOAT) return FLOAT;
    function SIN(X: LONG_FLOAT) return LONG_FLOAT;
end MATH_FUNCTIONS;
```

the package implementor can assure that when a user changes the representation of his floating point numbers (e.g., from FLOAT to LONG_FLOAT), he need not alter source text that uses the package MATH_FUNCTIONS[24].

4.1.2.2 Hierarchical Type Composition

One advantage that has been claimed for the derived type mechanism is that it provides a form of Simula's class concatenation[25]—the ability to build hierarchies of types, with each member of the hierarchy providing operations that are common to all higher members. However, the truly useful examples of class concatenation also add extra state. For example, consider the following example, adapted from one used by Dahl and Hoare:

```
class tree(val); integer val;
   begin
      ref(tree) left, right;
      procedure insert(x); integer x;
         comment Insert a node with value x in this tree,
                 if there is not one present;
      . . .
      ref(tree) procedure find(x); integer x;
         comment Return the subtree of this tree whose
                 root has val x, or none if there is none;
      . . .
   end of tree;
```

(Note: "**this** tree" in Simula refers to the tree of which the current instantiation of the routine invoking **this** is a member. The keyword **none** refers to the null pointer.) The class tree is now the top of a hierarchy; anything concatenated with it inherits the property of being an indexed collection of nodes that can be retrieved by key. Thus, after

---

[24] This, by the way, is an interesting example of how the overloading of function names provides a sort of database look-up facility; the compiler automatically finds the correct sine function to apply to get the desired precision

[25] Of which Dahl and Hoare provide a good description [Dahl 72].

```
tree class stock item;
   begin
      integer qoh, price, reorder point;
      . . .
```

`stock items` can be inserted and searched for. Note, however, that this example, which is typical of Simula, is not directly realizable in Ada with derived types, since the definition of `stock item` introduces extra state data (such as `price`) into the representation.

Thus, the utility of derived types in defining type hierarchies is limited to those cases where no state data needs to be concatenated. However, this is not a particularly interesting class of hierarchies. For example, in Dahl and Hoare's article there are no examples of Ada-style type concatenation.

4.1.2.3 "Poor Man's Strong Typing"

The phrase "poor man's strong typing" is the standard jargon for the definition of numeric types that are isomorphic to but distinct from the standard numeric types. A typical example is the one given at the beginning of this section:

```
type WEIGHT is new INTEGER;
type LENGTH is new INTEGER;
```

The programmer intends that `WEIGHT`s and `LENGTH`s can be added, subtracted, and multiplied by constants, but not that `WEIGHT`s can be added to `LENGTH`s. The declaration above does this, while declaring the two as subtypes of `INTEGER` would accomplish the first intent, but not the second.

Unfortunately, the derived type mechanism does only part of the job. For example, one is allowed to add a `LENGTH` to the product of two `LENGTH`s. On the other hand, one is not allowed to divide a `LENGTH` by a `TIME` to get a `VELOCITY` (where these are three distinct types). That is, derived types do not do dimensional analysis. Furthermore, it is possible to write a package that does true dimensional analysis without using derived types (see Appendix B, section B.1).

Historically, "poor man's strong typing" was a side-effect of the attempt to achieve portability of programs using numeric types, rather than a response to a perceived need to provide a way of differentiating arithmetically identical numeric types. Consequently, it is not clear whether the errors it might catch are at all common or bothersome. While the avoidance of such errors might be a nice side-effect of *having* derived types, it hardly serves as a justification for *adding* them to the language[26]. Indeed, in the new Pascal standard [Addyman 80], the authors do make all subranges of the type integer be distinct types, but then they substantially undo the effect by introducing a notion of assignment compatibility.

4.1.2.4 Change of Representation

This issue is somewhat of a straw man, actually. It involves the ability to write, e.g.,

```
type A is record ... end;
type B is new A;
pragma PACK(B);  -- or some other representation specification
x: A; y: B;
```

and thus to have

```
x := B(y);
```

be automatically defined to unpack the variable y into x. Since the functionality involved is so easily provided by a user-defined procedure (consisting of a sequence of assignments of corresponding fields), the desire to facilitate change of representation seems to be a rather insubstantial motivation for the derived type mechanism.

---

[26] In reporting on experience with the Mesa language, Geschke, Morris, and Satterthwaite cite one problem that derived numeric types might help [Geschke 77]. The authors noted that in Mesa, which is a system implementation language, programmers often used integers as both addresses and array indices in order to be able to do address arithmetic. This made it impossible for the compiler to pick up errors resulting from using a pointer as an array index (for example). The authors go on to suggest a facility that would allow the creation of distinct numeric types. However, the current Mesa language [Mitchell 78] seems to get on quite well by just extending some of the arithmetic operators to allow arithmetic between integers and pointers.

4.1.2.5 Constructing Private Types

Consider the following example of a using a derived type in defining a private type.

```
package A is
   type INT is private;
   function "+"(x,y: INT) return INT;

private
   type INT is new INTEGER;
end A;

package body A is
   function "+"(x,y: INT) return INT is
      begin  return INT(INTEGER(x)+INTEGER(y));  end;
end A;
```

In effect, the conversion operators, INTEGER(*) and INT(*) act as mappings between the representation type, INTEGER, and the defined type INT. We needed them in the implementation of " + " because the function A." + " hides the operation " + " that INT would otherwise inherit from INTEGER.

However, there is another approach to that does not require derived types (and which, in fact, was pointed out by the Ada design team [Ada 80]). That is to use a trivial record type:

```
 . . .
private
   type INT is record V: INTEGER; end;
end A;

package body A is
   function "+"(x,y: INT) return INT is
      begin  return (V => x.V + y.V);  end;
end A;
```

This appears to solve the problem entirely, without recourse to derived types. The inconvenience of writing, e.g., x . V rather than x and of using aggregates to denote values of type INT seems a small price to pay (indeed, the body of " + " happens to be shorter in the re-write), and this price is paid only in the body of the defining package, A.

One simple extension to Ada that retains virtually all of the notational convenience of the derived type solution is to allow private type declarations to be fulfilled by *subtype* declarations[27]:

```
 . . .
private
   subtype INT is INTEGER;
end A;

package body A is
   function "+"(x,y: INT) return INT is
      begin  return x STANDARD."+" y;  end;
end A;
```

Outside the package A, the type A.INT is a distinct type. Inside the package, however, it acts as a synonym for INTEGER. Note that the "+" operator used in the body of A must be qualified to avoid an infinite recursive regress. Naturally, when faced with a specification such as

```
package AMBIG is
   type INT is private;
   procedure F(x: INT);
   procedure G(x: INTEGER);
 . . .
```

the programmer has no choice but to use a record to represent the type **INT**.

4.1.3 Summary

What we have seen in this section is that the derived type mechanism, a rather complex piece of semantic machinery, provides nothing but some minor conveniences. Had we been given an Ada that initially contained no derived type mechanism at all, it is doubtful that we would have felt any particular need for to provide one. The largest chunk of notational convenience provided by derived types is probably in the definition of private types. As discussed in Section 4.1.2.5, however, a much simpler mechanism would suffice to provide the convenience.

---

[27] An extension that Habermann, et al. have also suggested [Habermann 79].

4.2 Simplifying by generalizing: Literals, Aggregates, and Assignment

The preceding section was devoted to the out-and-out excision of a language feature—specifically, to showing that the useful facilities provided by derived types are already present in other language features. In this section, we'll concentrate instead on adding facilities that expand the programmer's ability to define properties of private types. In particular, we will try to reduce the special status afforded the assignment operator and the various denotations of constants (literals and aggregates). In the process, we will, in fact, be able to simplify other parts of Ada, or at least increase the uniformity of their description. Section 4.3 will build on the work here to further simplify the language.

This example is intended to demonstrate an important point of this thesis: that it is feasible to formulate a von Neumann-style language's definitional mechanisms with sufficient generality—sufficient expressiveness—that we achieve a simpler language (one with a smaller kernel and a smaller set of concepts) without any particular sacrifice in such practical criteria as performance. We will formulate assignment in such a way that Ada's current semantics holds for all those cases where the user does not use his capability to define it—thus managing to avoid performance problems—while simplifying the language (in the net) by using the generalized definition to define existing pieces of the current semantics.

During the review of Ada, several reviewers suggested that it might be helpful if programmers could redefine certain of the primitive operators, most notably the assignment operator. Nassi even went so far as to give a partial design [Nassi 80]. The design developed in this section differs from his in several ways. The most important difference is that Nassi attempted to use re-definition of assignment alone to accomplish all the effects that we shall obtain with two separate facilities. Although it would be nice to minimize the number of new features involved, we will see that certain technical issues tend to complicate Nassi's approach when it is fully elaborated.

In terms of the criteria established in section 1.3, the ability to define assignment operators gives a programmer greater power to free his clients from details of his abstractions, particularly in those cases where the abstract operation of copying a value involves more that a simple representation copy. The use of assignment to define literals is a handy side-effect that allows programmers to define a richer set of notations.

4.2.1 Motivating Examples

Let's consider the `VString` type mentioned in Section 2.1. The idea is to capture the notion of a variable-length string variable, as in PL/1. In its simplest form, it has the following specifications:

```
subtype NATURAL0 is INTEGER range 0 .. INTEGER'LAST;

package Strings is
   type VString(MaxLen: NATURAL0) is private;
      -- The domain of VString(N) is all STRINGs with LENGTH<=N.

   function Conv(V: VString) return STRING;
   function Conv(S: STRING; MaxLen: NATURAL0 := 0)
         return VString;
      -- For all STRINGs S, Conv(Conv(S)) = S and
      --     Conv(S,N).MaxLen = MAX(N, S'LENGTH)
private        -- Representation

   type VString(MaxLen: NATURAL0) is
      record
         Len: NATURAL := 0;
         Val: STRING(1 .. MaxLen);
      end record;

end Strings;
```

Ideally, we would like `VStrings` to be able to perform operations such as

```
<<S1>> V1 := V2;            -- Copy string variable
<<S2>> V1 := "A";           -- Initialize V1 to the string "A"
<<S3>> V1 := V1 & " "       -- Append a blank to V1.
```

where `V1` and `V2` are two `VStrings`. But in general, these are difficult. In statement S1, the assignment will work (according to the semantics of revised Ada) only if V1 and V2 have the same *maximum* lengths, whereas we would prefer to check only that the length of the current value of V2 be less than the maximum length of V1. The right-hand side of statement S2 is a string and cannot be assigned to a VString. Finally, in statement S3, while "&" can certainly be overloaded to take a VString and a STRING, the assignment will only work if the *maximum* length of the value returned is equal to that of V1. For these reasons, VString is a less-than-perfect realization of the functionality we set out to capture.

When we look at implementation issues, furthermore, we see a few more troublesome points. For example, if Conv(V2)'LENGTH is 5 and its Pr[MaxLen] is 100, then the statement

```
V1 := V2;
```

need only copy 5 characters. But of course, it is rather unlikely that a compiler would ever recognize this; it is a piece of knowledge that the implementor has and is unable to convey to the compiler.

Now consider an obvious implementation of Conv:

```
function Conv(S: STRING; N: NATURAL) return VString is
      Result: VString(MaxLen => MAX(N, S'LENGTH));
   begin
      Result.Len := S'LENGTH;  Result.Val(1 .. S'LENGTH) := S;
      return Result;
   end;
```

Now this works well enough, and it is even conceivable that a good compiler would be able to compile

```
V1 := Conv("Short", V1.MaxLen);
```

into

```
V1.Len := 5;  V1.Val(1..5) := "Short";
```

(although this is a rather sophisticated optimization.) Note, though, an interesting side-effect: The operator " = " no longer does the expected (since in general that part of the Val field beyond the current length is garbage). The programmer can get around this by defining instead

```
function Conv(S: STRING; N: NATURAL) return VString is
   begin
      return (MaxLen => MAX(N, S'LENGTH), Len => S'LENGTH,
              Val => S & (S'LENGTH+1 .. MAX(N, S'LENGTH) => ' '));
   end;
```

but this, of course, forces the compiler to do a fair amount of unnecessary work setting the unused locations. This problem results, of course, from the special status of the "=" operator, which cannot be re-implemented in the case of the specification above.

All of this is to say that the original package specification cannot be fulfilled as well (i.e., with the performance) that we'd like, because Ada does not allow us to re-implement the operators "=" and ":=". In other words, the package should have looked like this:

```
package Strings2 is
   type VString(MaxLen: NATURAL0) is limited private;

   -- Conv functions as before

   function "="(X,Y: VString) return BOOLEAN;
   procedure Set(LHS: out VString; RHS: VString);
   procedure Set(LHS: out VString; RHS: STRING);

   . . .

end Strings2;
```

With these specifications, we can write the statements S1—S2 as follows:

```
<<S1>>  Set(V1, V2);
<<S2>>  Set(V1, "A");
<<S3>>  Set(V1, V1 & " ");
```

The operators Set and "=" can now be implemented to perform as we intended. We could argue that the use of Set instead of ":=" is a mere notational annoyance. For the most part, this is true, but there are a few other annoyances. If we wish to pass string literals to some function that takes an argument of type VString, we must still use an explicit Conv; the compiler doesn't "catch on" from the definition of Set that we intend to be able to use strings as literals. Furthermore, limited types are rather, well, limited in some rather important ways. It is impossible to define constants of type String2.VString or to use values of the type as part of an initial value in an allocator. Furthermore, any type containing such a VString inherits these same limitations.

None of the objections raised above constitute fatal problems. It would be wrong to add enormously to the semantics of Ada in order to remedy them. At the same time, what we have seen are arbitrary limitations on the ability of programmer to define notation or, having defined it, to implement it as he desires. The next task, therefore, is to see if the restrictions are necessary—if we can remove them without any net increase in the complexity of the Ada language.

4.2.2 Overview of Proposed Design

To summarize the discussion of the preceding section, what we'd like is a set of facilities that

- Allows a programmer—specifically a package designer—to specify and implement the operation "copy a value of (private) type T."

- Integrates this definition with the rest of the language (parameter passing, definition of constants) just as the primitive notion of "copy" for standard types is integrated.

- Provides a convenient notation for literals of a user-defined type.

Many approaches are possible. Here we will elaborate a proposal sketched by Nassi, that tries to solve both problems simultaneously by allowing multiple overloadings of a new definable operator, ":=" [Nassi 80]. By defining, for example,

```
procedure ":="(LHS: out VString; RHS: VString);
procedure ":="(LHS: out VString; RHS: STRING);
```

The programmer defining VStrings could arrange first, that the legality of

VString assignment depend only on the current length of RHS being no more than MaxLen of LHS, and second, that string constants be valid VString literals. These same ":=" operators would be used for passing parameters as well. Unfortunately, there is a slight technical difficulty with Nassi's proposal: It interacts poorly with current implementation schemes. Consider the following declaration and subsequent call:

```
procedure G(Z: VString) is
    . . .
G(". . .");
```

The quantity Z.MaxLen will presumably be supplied by ":=" when it is invoked for the assignment to Z. That is, the body of ":=" can accept unconstrained (indeed, unallocated) **VStrings** for its LHS argument and assign to them. Furthermore, this same capability must be extended to **out** parameters of any procedure.

By allocating VStrings on a heap, and treating assignment as an allocation operator, it is possible to implement these semantics[28]. However, my purpose here is to show enhancements that do *not* require any particular changes in the familiar implementation strategies—that are clearly minor modifications to the language. Therefore, we will take a different tack in attacking the implementation problem.

Several authors have addressed the problem of defining the external representation of types. Wallis has described an interesting language facility for the PPL language [Wallis 80]. His design allows a programmer to define a format for the external representation and conversions to and from this format. We will take the simpler approach (simpler from the language designer's point of view, admittedly) of merely providing the necessary

---

[28] Indeed, there would be advantages to taking this approach. In particular, the peculiar rules surrounding discriminants—they may not be used in expressions, they may be unconstrained only if given an initial value—could probably go away.

"hooks", leaving the interpretation of literals entirely up to the definer's program.

Again, the point of this exercise is not so much to produce a particular design as to demonstrate what we can accomplish by closer attention to abstraction mechanisms. However, for such a demonstration to be convincing, it must be rather detailed, lest it be dismissed with the irritating (but sometimes justified) claim that "you have not considered all the problems."

4.2.2.1 Assignment

The basic idea behind the steps that follow is to recast the assignment operation as an ordinary procedure. Ada already has a way of defining (or rather, undefining) the assignment operator: the limited private type. Since the point of our exercise is to install a general mechanism for defining the copying of values, it would be nice if we could encompass the existing mechanism in it, and this is what we'll do. A natural consequence will be that the equality operator, " = ", will also become an ordinary relational operator.

The following is a list of the major changes.

1. Remove the **limited** keyword and instead make all private types "limited" in the sense that they do not automatically export a ":=" or " = " operator.

2. Add ":=" as a definable binary operator and make the operator " = " an ordinary relational operator in all respects, eliminating the current restrictions on its argument and return types, in particular. The operator ":=" must be a procedure with two operands. It is treated as an ordinary binary operator having lowest precedence. An invocation

   ```
   A := B;
   ```

   is equivalent to

```
":="(A,B);
```

3. Define the operators ":=", "=", and "/=" implicitly on all scalar and access types, as in the current semantics. Likewise, define an implicit ":=" operator on any array or record type for which there is an ":=" operator visible for each component's type. These are component-wise assignments using the assignment operators defined on the components. They behave as in current Ada with respect to discriminants and index constraints.

4. An invocation of a ":=" operator is type-valid (i.e., is legal within the type system) if its two actuals have the same types as their corresponding formals. An invocation of any other subprogram is type-valid if each actual parameter has the same type as the corresponding formal or is *assignment compatible* with the formal. A parameter is assignment compatible if it is an **in** parameter and there is a unique ":=" operator visible at the point of call with the formal's type as the type of its left operand and the actual's type as the type of its right operand.

5. Unconstrained formal parameters inherit any discriminant constraints as in current Ada, except in the (formerly illegal) case where an unconstrained **in** parameter does not have the same type as its actual. In this case, the discriminants of the formal are set by the assignment operator.

6. Because of rule 5, some parameters to the assignment operator will have constraints that were formerly impossible—e.g., **in out** array parameters in which the actual parameter does not have an index constraint. As an implementation restriction, any such parameter may only be assigned to in the body of the assignment operator.

7. Parameters are passed to the ":=" operator by reference. Any constraints on the formals must equal those of the actuals. For

other subprograms, parameters that are assignment compatible, but not of equivalent type, are copied by the appropriate assignment operator (which must be visible at the point of call). Parameters that are of equivalent type may be passed by copy, using any assignment operator with the correct parameter types visible at either the call site or subprogram body. Parameters that are of equivalent type and constraints may be passed by reference. (These last two cases are just the extension of current Ada's ambiguity regarding passing by reference vs. passing by value).

These are the major changes. To support them, we also add a few minor ones:

- Outside the package containing it, an operator designator is always visible throughout its scope according to the rules for identifiers made visible by a **use** clause. (in contrast to an ordinary subprogram declaration, which if declared in a package specification, is only visible as a result of a **use** declaration or explicit qualification)[29].

- An explicit definition of ":=" within a package overrides any implicit definition of ":=" introduced by the full type declaration for the private type. For a type `T`, the notation `T'ASSIGN` is a synonym for any implicit assignment operator originally defined on it[30]

- Do not extend "=" automatically to array or record types, but

---

[29]The purpose of this change is first to make the visibility of ":=" be as in current Ada. Second, it seems a good idea in general; one generally does not want to have to qualify applications of operators.

[30]Thus, one can use the implicit definition in implementing the overriding definition within the body of a package.

define it on the pre-defined type STRING[31].

- Invoke the ":=" operator implicitly to initialize a variable or constant, to copy a value into an aggregate, and to copy an initial value into a record component.

Mostly, these changes constitute a re-formulation of Ada's description to treat ":=" as an ordinary subprogram. The changes to limited types and the "=" operator represent contractions. Although some complexity is added by having to allow for a user-defined copy for parameter passing, the increase is compensated by the fact that this new description explains certain parts of the current semantics, such as the conversion of numerics literals (which have "universal" types) to the appropriate numeric types, as we'll see in the next section.

Rule 6 is an implementation restriction imposed to avoid distributed overheads that would result from a radical change such as introducing unconstrained array variables. For example, consider

```
package P is
   type Vect1 is array (INTEGER range <>) of E;
   type Vect2 is array (INTEGER range <>) of E;
   procedure ":="(LHS: out Vect1; RHS: in Vect1);
end;
```

with a subsequent declaration

```
Z: constant Vect1 := some expression of type Vect2;
```

This eventually results in the having P.":=" instantiated with Z, which has no constraint. Nowhere else in the language is such a variable possible, and considerable difficulty would be involved in providing for the possibility in the general case. However, with rule 6, we can use the same (existing) mechanism as is used to return size-unresolved function results (e.g., the standard "&" operators, which return arrays of undetermined size.)

---

[31] Although this is a decrease in power over current Ada, it seems justified since "=" no longer has special status and comparison of general records and arrays for equality is not particularly common.

In sections to follow we will be using this proposed design.

4.2.2.2 Literals

A *literal* is a denotation of a value having the property that the value denoted can be computed given just the denotation itself (and the type of value required). Thus, a string of digits such as "1" or "10030" can be interpreted as an integer and there is an algorithm for converting any such string into an integer. The assignment operators presented above allow us to formulate this by saying that for any type, T, with literals, there is an assignment from literal denotations to T:

```
procedure ":="(LHS: out T; RHS: LITERAL_DENOTATION);
```

The type LITERAL_DENOTATION could be any type at all, including an array or record type with aggregates. This allows us to use STRINGs, for example, as literals of any type.

To allow us to write numbers without ugly quotation marks and to make numeric literals work, we add a few adjustments:

- There is a pre-defined type in STANDARD declared

  ```
  type NUMERIC_LITERAL is
     array (NATURAL range <>) of CHARACTER;
  ```

  Any numeric_literal, N, occurring in program text is equivalent to the aggregate NUMERIC_LITERAL'("N").

- Any pre-defined numeric types have ":=" operators defined going from NUMERIC_LITERAL to the numeric type that provide the necessary literals.

- To make qualification work as before, we'll say that if a qualified expression T'(E) is used as a value then it is valid if (E) can be interpreted as a T or if it is assignment compatible with T.

4.2.3 Examples

We can summarize the alternate design done in this section with two examples. First, we'll consider one last time the definition of the type `VString`. What we are after, again, is a type that behaves like the standard type `STRING`, but allows variables the size of whose contents may vary over the lifetime of the variable. The specification is given in Fig. 4-1 (the implementation is straightforward and is not shown). The specification provides literals, assignment, the standard lexicographical comparisons, and concatenation.

This specification gives us, among other things, the "ragged array":

```
TABLE: constant array (INTEGER range <>) of VString(MaxSize) :=
     ("DELETE", "FORWARD", "APPEND", "MAIL", "EXIT", "HEADERS");
```

As a second example, consider the problem of defining literals to denote sets. In current Ada, one can write

```
type SetOfInt is array (INT) of BOOLEAN;
```

to denote the type whose domain consists of sets of values of subtype `INT`. If `S` is a `SetOfINT` it represents the set of all `n` such that `S(n)`. The set {1, 7, 10, 13} is denoted

```
SetOfINT'(1 | 7 | 10 | 13 => TRUE, others => FALSE).
```

Could we arrange a better notation? Certainly; we define

```
type SetOfINTLiteral is array (INTEGER range <>) of INT;
procedure ":="(LHS: out SetOfINT; RHS: SetOfINTLiteral) is
   begin
      LHS := SetOfINT'(others => FALSE);
      for i in RHS'RANGE loop LHS(i) := TRUE end loop;
   end;
```

Now we can write (1, 7, 10, 13) to denote {1, 7, 10, 13}.

```
subtype NATURAL0 is INTEGER range 0 .. INTEGER'LAST;

package Strings3 is

   type VString(MaxLen: NATURAL0) is private;
      -- The domain of VString(N) is all STRINGs with LENGTH<=N.

-- Literals and conversion to external representation

   procedure ":="(LHS: out VString; S: STRING);
      -- Post condition: LHS.MaxLen = S'LENGTH if LHS not
      -- constrained.  LHS contains the abstract value S.
      -- Exception if S too long.
   function IMAGE(V: VString) return STRING;
      -- IMAGE(VALUE(s)) = s[32]

-- Assignment

   procedure ":="(x: out VString; y: VString);
      Copies y into x iff the string in y is in the domain of x.

-- Comparisons (have standard meanings, lexicographic comparison
-- of the abstract (STRING) values).

   function "="  (x,y: VString) return BOOLEAN;
   function "<"  (x,y: VString) return BOOLEAN;
   function ">"  (x,y: VString) return BOOLEAN;
   function "<=" (x,y: VString) return BOOLEAN;
   function ">=" (x,y: VString) return BOOLEAN;


-- Concatenation

   function "&"(x,y: VString) return VString;
      -- MaxLen of the result is the length of the concatenated
      -- values.  IMAGE(x & y) = IMAGE(x) & IMAGE(y).

-- etc.

private

   type VString(MaxLen: NATURAL0) is
      record
         Len: NATURAL := 0;
         Val: STRING(1 .. MaxLen);
      end record;

end Strings3;
```

Figure 4-1: Final `VString` (variable-length string) package.

[32] Any discrete type, T, in current Ada has a function `T'IMAGE` that converts T's to `STRING`s that could serve as literal denotations of their values.

4.2.4 Possible objections

When programmers are allowed control over what are normally built-in features, there is always a danger of unpleasant surprise. We expect, seeing X := Y, that X will have the value previously contained in Y. This expectation is destroyed, however, when some idiot defines

```
procedure ":="(LHS: out INTEGER; RHS: INTEGER) is
   begin STANDARD.":="(LHS, 0);  end;
```

Likewise, we expect that the literal 2 will always mean the integer that it traditionally denotes, but this expectation may also be destroyed when someone writes

```
procedure ":="(LHS: out INTEGER; RHS: NUMERIC_LITERAL) is
   begin  STANDARD.":="(LHS,59);  end;
```

It would be extremely difficult to fix this problem by hedging ":=" around with various restrictions, without also restricting the usefulness right out of it. Therefore, we'll leave it up to the programmer to insure that the effect of an assignment is to create a copy of the (abstract) value, with perhaps some "benign" side-effects. Definitions such as the two above are interesting pathologies. However, a definition of ":=" is a subprogram like any other and is subject to testing in isolation like any other. To do damage, furthermore, a re-definition must be in an inner scope; the sort of situation in which importing a library definition changes the meaning of one's entire program does not arise in Ada.

With regard to literals, one might naturally wonder about leaving syntax checking and range checking to a user's program. For simplicity, I have lumped all numeric literals together, assuming that their ":=" operators would assure valid use. The only general alternative seems to be to allow syntactic specification of literals, an extension that seems rather involved.

However, even though I may *describe* the semantics of INTEGER literals, for example, as if they involved a run-time conversion, nothing can keep my compiler from knowing about the more important, standard, literals and publishing warnings along the lines of "This will cause an exception if you evaluate it." The programmer gets the same information in any case. Indeed, with proper pragmas (such as INLINE and perhaps another that requests that a subprogram be executed at compile time), these same amenities can be made available to user-defined literals as well.

4.3 Real arithmetic

Arithmetic types are classic examples of data types in the now-traditional mold: domains of values together with operations on those domains. In this section, we explore what it would take to define certain of Ada's arithmetic types—the real types—within Ada itself; that is, within a package. With one minor exception, we will use only the facilities provided in the preceding sections.

The point of this exercise is to complete the demonstration begun in Section 4.2. There, we introduced "lateral" changes—modifications that slightly generalize Ada's definitional capabilities. Now we demonstrate the possibilities. In particular, we consider the "real types" in Ada—the built-in types for doing arithmetic on rational numbers—and show how these can be re-formulated as run-of-the-mill private types in a package. That is, we show how generalizing the definitional capabilities of a language (perhaps introducing some local complexity) allows us to simplify the its overall semantics.

This is an interesting exercise from a practical point of view. The fixed point types in particular (those in which the fractional point occupies a fixed position with respect to the last significant digit) are a fairly special-purpose facility, having been included for the benefit of fairly old hardware designs where floating point was not economically feasible. Yet, fixed point types, at the moment, are a necessary part of the Ada language, built into each compiler. Finally, the semantics of fixed point types in current Ada has been a source of numerous problems (it fits poorly with the type mechanism). For that matter, floating point arithmetic—and the need for it—aren't universal either.

It is attractive to consider building a compiler without these arithmetic facilities, and adding them in the form of packages (written entirely in Ada, possibly with occasional forays into machine code to take advantage of hardware instructions). Not only does this partition and simplify the task of compiler-writing, but it also allows such things as local re-implementations of real arithmetic that provide "infinite" precision or various instrumentation.

There are several reasons one might give for eschewing this rosy prospect in favor of building in the syntax and semantics of some particular set of arithmetic types:

- *Appearance*: a built-in notation can be tailored to be clean, concise, and convenient.
- *Functionality:* if a language lacks sufficient definitional capability, it may be impossible to get certain effects (while hiding the mechanism, that is).
- *Efficiency:* to define the desired package, one might be forced to use constructs so general that the compiler would require specialized knowledge to do a decent job of code generation, so that one might just as well build the features in anyway.

The are the concerns we must address for any proposed use of Ada's abstraction mechanisms—current and proposed—to implement real arithmetic.

We'll begin, in the next section, with a review of the existing real arithmetic facilities in Ada. Next, Section 4.3.2 will give the packages specifying the proposed definition. Section 4.3.3 will consider the issues raised above for the resulting definition.

4.3.1 Overview of real types

Ada's real arithmetic[33] is divided into two parts, fixed point and floating point. The latter is probably familiar, so let's just briefly review the former.

The term "fixed point arithmetic" refers to approximate arithmetic of rational numbers in which each arithmetic operations produces results whose absolute error is bounded by some fixed value, called the "delta" or "step size". The intention behind such arithmetic, from a programmer's point of view, is to provide a sort of "poor man's floating point", often using integer arithmetic with an implicit implicit binary point being maintained by the compiler. The requirements set on Ada by STEELMAN for a fixed point facility were

1. That the language provide decimal literals (item 2G in the STEELMAN Requirements [DoD 78]).

2. That the language provide the standard operations for arithmetic and for comparison of numeric values (3-1B).

3. That the ranges, precisions, and step sizes of each numeric variable be specifiable (indeed, required) (3-1C, 3-1D, 3-1G).

4. That the semantics be sufficiently flexible to allow direct use of the underlying hardware (firmware) on most machines (an

---

[33] A term that makes us mathematicians writhe.

efficiency consideration). Also that the underlying characteristics of the hardware—notably actual precisions, radices, exponent ranges—be obtainable by the program through environmental inquiries (3-1E).

5. That explicit conversions not be required for arithmetic or assignment between variables of differing scales, precisions, or ranges (3-1D, 3-1G, 3-1H).

6. That fixed point arithmetic be exact: that is, that the step size be well-defined and that arithmetic obey precisely the rules for doing arithmetic on numbers with given absolute precisions (3-1F).

The Ada designers in effect ignored the last two requirements, treating fixed point numbers as "approximate" in the sense that the declared step size merely bounds the actual step size, and that explicit conversions are required between types with differing step sizes[34] except for multiplications and divisions of operands with differing fixed types.

To summarize the resulting semantics, Ada provides the following numeric types:

- *Integer types:*[35] The implementation provides some number of underlying integer types, one of which is called `INTEGER`. Integer types may be constrained with a range constraint, as in

  ```
  X: INTEGER range 0 .. 255;
  ```

  or

  ```
  subtype MY_CODE is INTEGER range 0 .. 255;
  ```

  That is, the integer types are parameterized by range.

---

[34] No explicit conversion is required between different *subtypes* of the same fixed point types. The utility of having a subtype whose step size differs (is larger than) that of the base type, however, is highly questionable for various technical reasons.

[35] With both integer and floating types, I do not discuss automatic selection of underlying types on the basis of declared range. See Section 4.1.

The usual arithmetic operations are defined for each integer types, but not across types. The integer literals (which are built into the lexical structure of the language) are of an "unmentionable" type, which is denoted UNIVERSAL_INTEGER for purposes of exposition. An expression of this type is implicitly converted to whatever integer type is required by the containing context. The built-in arithmetic operations are overloaded on type UNIVERSAL_INTEGER. It is intended that this type have a domain larger than that of any of the "mentionable" integer types.

Each integer type or subtype allows inquiry of the limits of its range by pre-defined attributes. There are explicit conversion operators automatically defined between any two integer types in particular, and numeric types in general (denoted by a function bearing the name of the target type).

- *Fixed point types:* These have domains of the form

$$D = \{ x \mid x = n \cdot d, n \text{ an integer in } [L, U] \}$$

for some integers L and U and positive constant d[36]. A fixed point type is introduced by a declaration of the form

```
type FIXED is delta d' range L' .. U';
```

which specifies a superset of the domain D above if $L' <= L \cdot d$, $U' >= U \cdot d$, and $d' <= d$.

The operations provided are addition and subtraction of operands of one type and multiplication and division among *arbitrary* fixed types and integers. Multiplication and division of two fixed values yields a result of the unmentionable type UNIVERSAL_FIXED, which must be coerced by transfer functions into some user-

[36]The notation [a, b] denotes the closed interval {x | a <= x <= b}.

declared type before it can be used further[37].

The real literals, which cover both fixed and floating types, have a type UNIVERSAL_REAL, analogous to the type UNIVERSAL_INTEGER. The standard operators for absolute value, unary minus, addition, subtraction, multiplication, and division apply to UNIVERSAL_REAL, as well as multiplication, division, and exponentiation of a UNIVERSAL_REAL by a UNIVERSAL_INTEGER. The domain of type UNIVERSAL_REAL includes those of all user-definable real types.

- *Floating point types*: As with the integer types, an Ada implementation provides some set of floating point types of various precisions, including one called FLOAT. A programmer may constrain variables of a floating point type as to their range and precision, as in

```
y: FLOAT digits 10 range 0.0 .. 1.0;
subtype Probability is digits 10 range 0.0 .. 1.0;
```

The usual arithmetic operators are defined on operands of the same floating point type, or with one operand of type UNIVERSAL_REAL. There are attribute inquiries on floating point types and subtypes for range, implemented precision, and so forth.

[37] The reasons for these possibly odd-sounding semantics are that arithmetic among values with differing step sizes is necessary in practice; that each different step size requires a new type; and finally that explicit conversions implemented as simple arithmetic shifts will work for addition and subtraction, but are rather inconvenient for multiplication, as they often cause unnecessary overflows. I believe, however, that a somewhat less naive view of how to implement conversions among fixed point types would allow the somewhat cleaner semantics of requiring both operands to a multiplication to be of the same type.

4.3.2 Defining fixed point types

As a basis for definition, let's assume only the existence of the type INTEGER (possibly along with LONG_INTEGER, and whatever other standard types the implementation provides)[38]. Figure 4-2 gives a possible set of specifications for a fixed point type. Instead of using a "delta" value to specify the grain, this definition explicitly assumes a power-of-two model, which seemed to be the prevailing favorite among the designers in any case. A type UNIVERSAL (abstractly, a subset of the rationals) is introduced purely to prevent recursion in the definition. The example sneakily assumes that the type UNIVERSAL may be used as a discriminant constraint. Currently, Ada requires discriminant constraints to be scalar types, for no particularly good reason. The division operation returns a type QUOTIENT (also having a subset of the rationals as its domain) which must be qualified to be useful. This parallels the semantics of current Ada.

4.3.3 Discussion

The numeric properties of the package defined in Fig. 4-2 would be identical to those of current Ada's fixed point types. The FixedPoint package avoids the sticky problem of explaining cross-type multiplication (i.e., the multiplication (division) of values of two different fixed point types, which is necessary in current Ada because each delta must correspond to a distinct type) by having precisely one type. The implementations of FixedPoint would all be specified as in-line procedures. When combined with constant folding, this insures that the code produced by the compiler will be the same as that produced for current Ada, given corresponding programs; scaling can be computed at compile time.

---

[38]We could explore the possibility of foregoing a built in type INTEGER as well, but the type is sufficiently universal that there seems little need to make it "prunable". Furthermore, it is built into such things as the **for** loop and is likely to be rather difficult to remove.

```
package FixedPoint is
   type UNIVERSAL is private; -- Rationals
   type FIXED(Low,High: UNIVERSAL; DeltaScale:INTEGER);
      --Domain is the set {x | Low <= x = k*2^-DeltaScale <= High}

   procedure ":="(LHS: out FIXED; RHS: FIXED);
      -- Standard copy.  Requires that RHS satisfy bounds of LHS
      -- and that DeltaScales match.
   procedure ":="(LHS: out FIXED; RHS: NUMERIC_LITERAL);
      -- Literals of type FIXED.
   procedure ":="(LHS: out UNIVERSAL; RHS: NUMERIC_LITERAL);
      -- Literals of type UNIVERSAL (the only operation on them)

   function "+"(x,y: FIXED) return FIXED;
   function "-"(x,y: FIXED) return FIXED;
   function "*"(x,y: FIXED) return FIXED;
   type QUOTIENT is private;
   function "/"(x,y: FIXED) return QUOTIENT;
   function "**"(x: FIXED; y: INTEGER) return FIXED;

-- Coercions

   function Scale(x: QUOTIENT; Delta: INTEGER) return FIXED;
      -- Return x but with Delta for its exponent.
      -- Abstract value is the same.
   function Scale(x: FIXED; Delta: INTEGER) return FIXED;
   function Widen(x: INTEGER; Delta: INTEGER) return FIXED;
   function Trunc(x: FIXED) return INTEGER;

   function "<"(x,y: FIXED) return BOOLEAN;
   etc.

end FixedPoint;
```

Figure 4-2: A package providing fixed-point arithmetic.

The notation employed by a programmer using `FixedPoint` is on the same level as for current Ada. True, one specifies different things—the number of fractional binary places rather than the value of the smallest place—but this should make no difference in practice, since current practice is to deal in terms of number of fractional digits.

4.4 Subprogram values

This section and Section 4.5 discuss our final, and perhaps most significant, exploratory extension of Ada's definitional facilities—the *subprogram type*. By "subprogram type," I mean a type whose values are Ada subprograms (functions or procedures). This sort of feature is familiar to Lisp programmers, who use list values to denote Lisp functions, as well as to PL/1 and Algol 68 programmers. It is considerably less familiar to FORTRAN, Pascal, and Algol 60 programmers, although these languages do allow subprograms to be passed as (constant) parameters to subprograms (but not as variables). In Ada, due to a STEELMAN requirement ([DoD 78], paragraph 5D), subprogram values are illegal except as generic parameters—i.e., except as parameters to generic packages that are expanded statically "at compile time." Presumably, the intent of this requirement was to provide a minimal facility that would allow such things as numeric integration routines that take the functions to be integrated as an argument.

The purpose of the exercise undertaken in this section is to provide another demonstration of the feasibility and advantages of expressiveness in the definitional facilities of a language. Subprogram values are a particularly rich definitional primitive, even in the restricted form we introduce here. They make it possible to formulate parts of existing Ada—tasking, especially—in such a way that they can be provided as packages, thus becoming "optional" parts of the language (as happened to fixed point types in section 4.3), which can be provided in different forms, as fit the applications and architectures addressed by a particular implementation.

The feasibility of the facility (that is, its various costs relative to the current Ada design) derives from two sources. First, as a result of the requirement for a minimal form of parameterization by subprograms, a good deal of complexity was built into the generic mechanism to provide a static version of subprogram values. Hence, a good deal of the semantic mechanism—particularly the various rules involving compatibility of subprograms with subprogram specifications—is already present in current Ada. Second, we'll restrict ourselves to the relatively simple problem of providing "downward funargs," subprogram values that are valid only within the extent of the objects they access. This particular form of subprogram value is nothing new, even in von Neumann languages (PL/1 and Mesa are examples). Despite its limitations, it is definitionally powerful, as we shall see.

Our approach will be to introduce subprogram types with a new kind of type constructor (in addition to **array**, **record**, etc.) and then to revise other parts of Ada, notably generic definitions, to take advantage of the change. Section 4.5 will then apply this design to a re-formulation of Ada's tasking. The major issues to be addressed in this section are first, the smooth integration of subprogram types into Ada's type structure, and second, the "FUNARG problem"—the classical question of what environment is to be used for binding global variables in a subprogram value. This second problem is perhaps that most important, because of its potential distributed effect upon run-time overheads, and because of the safety issue: the possibility of accessing variables after termination of their extent. Again, the intent of these sections is to show how, by increasing the expressive power of a language, we can simplify it and its description.

4.4.1 Proposed Design

Ada uses what is called "name equivalence" for defining the equivalence of types. That is, for each type in a compilation unit, there is a declaration associating a unique identifier with that type, and two objects have equivalent types (for purposes of checking the semantic validity of subprogram calls) if they have been declared using this identifier for their type. The alternative, used in such languages as Algol 68, is *structural equivalence*, in which two types (modes, in Algol 68's terminology) are equivalent if they have isomorphic declarations, in a certain, well-defined sense.

The consistent use of name equivalence lends a certain uniformity to the Ada definition. Unfortunately, name equivalence is a rather inconvenient rule to apply to subprogram types. Part of this is custom. For example, we are used to seeing

```
function F(x: INTEGER) return INTEGER is ...
```

rather than something like

```
type F_TYPE is function (x: INTEGER) return INTEGER;
F: constant F_TYPE := ... ;
```

In other words, we are accustomed to identifying the type of a subprogram name with the argument signature of that subprogram.

More importantly, with name equivalence for subprogram types, there are name-management problems similar to those encountered with arrays. If two separate and independent modules provide operations on arrays, then, to be used together, there has to be some agreement as to precisely what is the type of the values they manipulate. They cannot be specified to operate on "any array of integers," but rather on objects of some named array type. It is possible to use generics to get around the problem, but the result is still somewhat awkward. We can anticipate a similar difficulty with a name equivalence rule for subprogram types.

With these considerations in mind, we can lay out a design in which subprogram types obey a structural equivalence rule. This rule turns out to be the same as Ada's current rule for generic formal subprograms, which, incidentally, already obey a structural equivalence rule in Revised (and Preliminary) Ada.

1. The syntax for type_mark is changed to

type_mark ::= *type*_name | *subtype*_name
| subprogram_type

2. A subprogram_type is essentially a subprogram specification, slightly modified:

subprogram_type ::=
procedure [formal_part]
| **function** [formal_part] **return** subtype_indication

3. The operation ":=" is defined implicitly on each functional type, but "=" is not. The effect of the assignment is to make the assigned-to variable refer to the subprogram value of the right operand, but with parameter names and default values as given for the declaration of the left operand. This same replacement of parameter names and default values occurs to a subprogram value returned as the result of a function call.

4. A named constant of a subprogram type may be deferred, just as can a constant of a private type[39]. A complete definition must appear later in the same declarative part (where, for this purpose, the body and private part of a package are considered to be in the same declarative part as the visible part).

5. The literals of a subprogram type are unlabeled blocks:

---

[39] Things would be simpler if *any* constant could be deferred in this fashion, but I will stick to the policy of changing no more than is necessary.

*subprogram*_constant ::=

```
[declare
   declarative_part]
begin
   sequence_of_statements
[exception
   {exception_handler} ]
end
```

The same block may designate subprograms of several different subprogram types. The type must be determined from surrounding context, without reference to the text of the literal. Any free variables in the subprogram constant are bound in the context in which the constant is elaborated (i.e., not at the point the subprogram denoted is eventually called). Note that the rules stated so far combine with existing parts of the language to provide fully qualified subprogram constants (what a Lisp programmer would call lambda expressions), as in

```
function (x: INTEGER) return INTEGER'(begin return x+1; end)
```

which denotes the successor function on the type INTEGER.

6. The declaration

```
procedure identifier [ formal_part ] is
      declarative_part
begin
   . . .
end [ designator ];
```

is an alternate form of

```
identifier: constant procedure [ formal_part ] :=
               declare
                  declarative_part
               begin
                  . . .
               end [ designator ];
```

and likewise for functions.

7. Two instances of subprogram_type denote the same type if the sequence of subtypes of the formal parts (in order) are pairwise identical, and the return types, if any, denote the same subtype.

8. Calling a subprogram object that has an assigned value proceeds as does a call in current Ada. Calling a subprogram object without a defined value raises an exception (UNDEFINED_SUBPROGRAM). As in current Ada, names of subprogram objects may be overloaded and resolved by context.

9. It is illegal to call a subprogram value when an object referenced in that subprogram value has been de-allocated.

10. Subprogram designators (such as "+") are legal as identifiers in object declarations (allowing, e.g.,
```
":=" : procedure (x: out T; y: T);)
```

Let's consider an example that will be of some use later on. Suppose that we have two packages, declared as follows

```
package OldStyleServer is
   procedure Write(Mssg: MessageType; Id: out MessageId);
   function Read(Id: MessageId) return MessageType;
end;

package NewStyleServer is
   procedure Write(Mssg: MessageType; Id: out MessageId);
   function Read(Id: MessageId) return MessageType;
end;
```

Notice that both of these packages have the same interface. Suppose that we have a program that would like to access these two servers uniformly but is indifferent about, indeed ignorant of which type of server is processing any given request. Such a situation arises in certain telecommunications applications, where equipment (and the software that supports it) with a long lifetime is replaced, piece by piece, with newer equipment. At any time, the two types of equipment co-exist.

We can reflect this by abstracting the common interface, as follows:

```
type Interface is
   record
      Write: procedure (Mssg: MessageType; Id: out MessageId);
      Read: function (Id: MessageType) return Mssg;
   end record;
```

A package that presents a uniform set of servers might now look like what is shown in Fig. 4-3.

```
package Service is
   function SelectServer return Interface;
      -- Return the interface of some server
end Service;

package body Service is

-- various data

   function SelectServer return Interface is
   begin
      if new kind selected then
         return (NewStyleServer.Write, NewStyleServer.Read);
      else
         return (OldStyleServer.Write, OldStyleServer.Read);
      end if;
   end;
end Service;
```

Figure 4-3: Example of an interface.

A program using this package first acquires an interface:

```
MyInterface: constant Interface := SelectServer();
```

so that his calls become

```
MyInterface.Write(M,Name);
Result := Read(Name);
```

In effect, the declaration of `MyInterface` is a declaration of a *virtual package* that is used much as is an ordinary package.

4.4.2 FUNARGS

The last items in the design above—concerning the binding of free identifiers and the scope of assigned-to variables—require some discussion. The issue of which context to use to bind free names—generally called the FUNARG problem—crops up in many languages and has many solutions. The Lisp language binds any name dynamically (i.e., to the last value bound to that name and not yet unbound). This solution is totally unfeasible in an Algol-style, block structured language such as Ada. The rule given above uses lexical scoping (binding depends on textual context), which is essentially the current semantics of Ada.

The restrictions on the calling of subprogram values are meant to eliminate cases such as

```
X: procedure;
function P1 return procedure is
   i: INTEGER;
   procedure P2 is begin i := i+1; end;
begin
   return P2;
end;
  . . .
X := P1;  X;
```

which cause the variable `P1.i` to get referenced after it is gone. The rule is more liberal than that in Algol 68, and allows subprogram values to be stored in variables with a greater lifetime. This avoids a number of rather annoying circumlocutions and makes implementations such as those in Section 4.4.5 possible.

4.4.3 Resulting simplifications of generics

As of a result of our new formulation of subprogram values, we can simplify generic procedure parameters rather drastically, essentially eliminating them. Instead of

```
generic
   type T is private;
   with function F(x: T) return T;
   with procedure G(x: T) := H;
    . . .
```

we can write

```
generic
   type T is private;
   F: function (x: T) return T;
   G: procedure (x: T) := H;
    . . .
```

Of course, all we've really done here is put what used to be filed under generics into subprogram types. But, after all, it was the original intent to make the introduction of subprogram types be as much a "lateral" move as possible; we've shown that a niche already exists for subprogram values in current Ada.

More precisely, the syntax for generic_formal_parameter becomes

generic_formal_parameter :: =
    parameter_declaration;
  | identifier_list: [**in**] subtype_indication := <>;
  | **type** identifier [discriminant_part] **is** generic_type_definition;

where the <> notation is interpreted as before: Generic parameters having a default value specified "<>" that are left unspecified in a generic instantiation are replaced by the value of a visible object with the same identifier in the instantiating context (if one exists and is unique).

We can go further than this, in fact. The various elaborations of generic_type_definitions that were added to PAda were a response to an annoying notational problem. Suppose that we want to have a package that defines some familiar mathematical operations on arrays. Naturally, we want this to work for any kind of array, so we write a generic definition:

```
generic
   type ElementType is private;
   type Vector is private;
   Zero: ElementType;   -- The zero element
   "+","*": function (x,y: ElementType) return ElementType := <>;
package VectorPackage is
   function DotProduct(x,y: Vector) return ElementType;
    . . .
```

Well, so far so good, but now we try to implement:

```
package body VectorPackage is

   function DotProduct(x,y: Vector) return ElementType is
         Result: ElementType := Zero;
      begin
         for i in Vector'RANGE
            loop  Result := x(i)*y(i) + Result;  end loop;
         return Result;
      end;
   . . .
```

Unfortunately, this we cannot do, for there is insufficient information in the generic header to indicate that `Vector` is an array type having the `RANGE` attribute, having elements of type `ElementType`, subscripting, and so forth.

Therefore, the revised language has ways of saying that a certain type is an array type, scalar type, and so forth.

Another possible approach, however, is to keep the simple model of PAda and simply make it easier to specify the necessary operations. This involves specifying the semantics of pre-defined type generators (**array**, **access**, (...), and so forth) in terms of a set of subprograms that they implicitly define. Next, we can introduce some convenient abbreviations for the appropriate subprogram types. Thus, we say that a type must have assignment on it by writing

```
":=": procedure (LHS: out T; RHS: T);
```

in the generic header. As an abbreviation, we can say that for any type T, the construct `T'ASSIGN_TYPE` is equivalent to

```
procedure (LHS: out T; RHS: T).
```

By enumerating a set of similar standard subprogram types, we can explain the semantics of the elaborate generic types without adding new types of construct to the language. For example, if T is an array type, declared

```
type T is array (INT range <>) of E;
```

then the following subprograms are introduced by its declaration:

```
function ArrayIndex(x: T; i: INT) return E;
   -- x(i) = ArrayIndex(x,i)
procedure ArraySet(x: in out T; i: INT; y: E);
   -- ArraySet(x,i,y) has the effect x(i) := y
function FIRST(x: T) return INT;
function LAST(x: T) return INT;
function LENGTH(x: T) return INTEGER;
```

4.4.4 Implementation considerations

Implementing subprogram values to get the desired functionality is not difficult. Perhaps the easiest approach is that used in, for example, Mesa [Mitchell 78]. A subprogram value consists of a pointer to the code of the subprogram and a pointer to the outermost stack frame that includes all global objects directly used by the subprogram. As in Algol 68, the compiler can make this determination statically. The display of stack frames is maintained through a static link in each stack frame. For an instantiation of a block, *B*, this link points to the innermost dynamically enclosing instantiation of the block lexically enclosing *B*.

The chief difficulty with the proposed semantics is that of checking the validity of the subprogram calls. We could simply declare that, like illegal use of aliasing or of the FREE operation, this particular error—calling a subprogram whose context has vanished—is not checked for. This is the attitude that Mesa takes, and it has a certain appeal. Still, we might hope to do better.

One feasible approach is to link together all subprogram variables that contain values with a given stack frame pointer. A variable is linked in when assigned to and removed from a list when de-allocated or re-assigned. Upon exit from a block, all procedural variables on that block's list are chased down and set to some invalid value. No such treatment need be given ordinary procedure constants.

4.4.5 Exception handling

So far, we have considered an alternate formulation of subprogram parameters in Ada and have tried to show that the complexity of its description and implementation, relative to current Ada, is acceptable. As an example of the proposed formulation and as a further justification of it, we now look at how it allows us to extend exceptional condition handling in Ada.

Ada's exception mechanism is a fairly simple control structure that allows exit from a dynamic nest of blocks and subprograms to a handler provided by a caller. It is, in other words, a "controlled **goto**," passing no information (aside from the identity of the exception) to the handler from the statement that raises the exception, and allowing no return from the handler to that statement. These limitations have drawn some fire from those who see the exception mechanism as something more than a device for blasting oneself out of an untenable situation. For example, we might want a handler that can take corrective or diagnostic action, resuming the failing operation when this action is complete. Levin's proposals for exception handling mechanisms [Levin 77], in fact, are formulated entirely in terms of this sort of control structure—in which the control flow of the signaler is not disrupted by the handler.

To see what subprogram values can do for us, let's start with a relatively simple and unambitious definition. Suppose that we want to provide a set of definitions so that a user can define something we'll call a *condition* (which in this section should be treated as short for "exceptional condition"). For any condition, the user must be able to associate a handler for that condition with a block, and to invoke the dynamically innermost handler for the condition. When the handler is finished, it is to return like an ordinary procedure call. Were we to install this as part of the Ada language *per se,* its syntax might resemble that of exceptions, as shown in part (a) of Fig. 4-4. The intent there is for the execution of **signal** in G to cause S5 to execute, after which execution continues with S2. No amount of package-defining, of course, is going to get us this syntax. However, we can get something that is "lexically homomorphic," as shown in part (b) of Fig. 4-4.

The package specification corresponding to part (b) of the figure is as follows.

```
E: condition;

procedure G is
   begin  S1; signal E; S2;  end;

procedure F is
   begin
      S3; G; S4;
   condition
      when E => S5;
   end;
```

(a) Built-in version

```
package E is new Condition;

procedure G is
   begin  S1; E.Signal; S2; end;

procedure F is
   begin
   E.Enable(begin
               S3; G; S4;
            end,
            Handler => begin  S5;  end);
   end;
```

(b) Using a generic package

Figure 4-4: Simple resumable exceptions: possible syntax.

```
generic package Condition is
   subtype HandlerType is procedure;
   subtype BodyType is procedure;

   procedure Signal;
      -- Invoke dynamically innermost handler established by
      -- Enable.  Has no effect if there is no handler.
   procedure Enable(BodyPart: BodyType; Handler: HandlerType);
      -- Execute BodyPart, first establishing Handler as the
      -- handler for Signals.

   -- Note: An instantiation of Condition may not be shared
   -- among multiple tasks.
end Condition;
```

Figure 4-5 gives the body for this first `Condition` package. In effect, the implementation creates a stack of "frames"—constructed from the handler procedures passed to `Enable`—with its top in the global variable[40] `CurrentFrame` and with its other elements stored in the constants called `LastFrame` in each nested instantiation of `Enable`. When `Enable` is called, it saves the previous frame, constructs a new frame from the handler provided, and pushes this on the stack. When an instantiation of `Enable` terminates (normally or by an exception) it pops the stack by restoring the previous value of `CurrentFrame`. Each frame temporarily restores the previous frame so that `Signals` within its handler will propagate out to the next frame as they should, rather than re-invoking the same frame. This implementation strongly resembles that used for the **signal** and **enable** constructs in the BLISS-11 language [Digital 74].

This example illustrates a subtle contrast between the design of subprogram values proposed here with that in Algol 68. In Algol 68, the definition above would not have worked: The variable `CurrentFrame` has an extent that is wider than any of its values. Even though the subprograms it contains would always be called legally, therefore, they could never be assigned to it in the first place.

The definition given is most awkward to use when there are multiple conditions that may be signaled. Suppose that we want to increase the functionality of the package to allow the sort of multiple handler specification illustrated in part (a) of Fig. 4-6. Again, we cannot, in fact, use this suggestive syntax, but we can get something similar, as shown in part (b) of the figure. In this revised facility, conditions have become values of the type `Condition`, and the `Enable` procedure gets passed an array of handler associations. The function `Init` creates new values of the type `Condition`. Within any of these handlers, the condition that caused the handler to be invoked is bound to the

---

[40] Global in extent, that is, not scope.

```
package body Condition is
   subtype FrameType is procedure;
   CurrentFrame: FrameType :=
      begin  null;  end;  -- Default action

   procedure Enable(BodyPart: BodyType; Handler: HandlerType)
   is
      LastFrame: constant FrameType := CurrentFrame;
      procedure NewFrame is
         begin
            CurrentFrame := LastFrame;
            Handler;
            LastFrame := CurrentFrame;
         exception -- Make sure frame pointer restored
            others => LastFrame := CurrentFrame;
         end NewFrame;
   begin -- Body of Enable
      CurrentFrame := NewFrame;   -- Establish handler
      BodyPart;
      CurrentFrame := LastFrame;
   exception -- Make sure frame pointer restored
      others => CurrentFrame := LastFrame;
   end Enable;

   procedure Signal is
      begin  CurrentFrame;  end;

end Condition;
```

Figure 4-5: Implementation of simple condition package.

name `CurrentCondition`. The special name `OTHERWISE` is analogous to the keyword **others**.

Figure 4-7 shows a possible specification for this facility. To account for sets of conditions (for example, `E2 or E3`) the specification introduces the type `ConditionSet`. The `OTHERWISE` condition is then simply a constant of this type. Note the overloading of ":=" used to allow `Condition` values to be coerced to type `ConditionSet`. In this specification, I have not bothered to require that a condition appear exactly once in a set of associations, although production version, one would probably want to do so.

Figure 4-8 shows an implementation of the specifications given in Fig. 4-7 (i.e., the body of the package and a private part giving the representations of private types). Essentially, the implementation is precisely the same as in

```
E1,E2,E3: condition;

procedure G is
   begin  S1; signal E2; S2;  end;

procedure F is
   begin
      S3; G; S4;
   condition
      when E1 => S5;
      when E2 | E3 => S6;
      when others => S7; signal;
   end;
```

(a) Built-in version

```
use Conditions;
E1: constant Condition := Init();
E2: constant Condition := Init();
E3: constant Condition := Init();

procedure G is
   begin  S1; Signal(E2); S2; end;

procedure F is
   begin
   Enable(begin
             S3; G; S4;
          end,
          Handler => (
             E1 > begin  S5;  end,
             E2 or E3 > begin  S6;  end,
             OTHERWISE >
                begin  S7; Signal(CurrentCondition);  end));
   end;
```

(b) Using the `Conditions` package

Figure 4-6: Possible syntax for more elaborate signals.

Fig. 4-5, but each frame now searches for the handler to use. Values of type `ConditionSet` are represented as vectors of boolean values, so that the implicit definition of **or**—component-wise inclusive "or"—serves as the implementation of the **or** operator.

Further elaborations are possible. For example, it is quite straightforward to extend `Signal` so that it can pass an item of data along to the handler. The

```
generic
   MaxConditions: NATURAL;
      -- Maximum legal number of Condition values
package Conditions is
   type Condition is private;
   function Init return Condition;
      -- Returns a new Condition.  Causes CONSTRAINT_ERROR if
      -- there would then be more than MaxConditions
      -- Conditions.
   procedure ":="(LHS: out Condition; RHS: Condition);

   type ConditionSet is private;
      -- Domain: sets of values of type Condition
   procedure ":="(LHS: out ConditionSet; RHS: Condition);
      -- Set LHS to the set containing RHS.
   procedure ":="(LHS: out ConditionSet; RHS: ConditionSet);
   function "or"(X,Y: ConditionSet) return ConditionSet;
      -- X or Y is the union of X and Y.
   OTHERWISE: constant ConditionSet;
      -- The set containing all Conditions

   subtype BodyType is procedure;
   subtype HandlerType is
      procedure (CurrentCondition: Condition);

   type Assoc is
      record CS: ConditionSet; H: HandlerType;  end record;
   function ">"(CS: ConditionSet; H: HandlerType) return Assoc;
      -- CS > H yields the record Assoc'(CS,H).
   type HandlerList is array (INTEGER range <>) of Assoc;
      -- A value of type HandlerList specifies a mapping between
      -- Conditions and bodies.  If a given Condition appears in
      -- more than one Assoc, the first applies.
   procedure Signal(C: Condition);
      -- Invoke innermost enclosing handler for C established by
      -- a call to Enable.
   procedure Enable(BodyPart: BodyType; Handlers: HandlerList);
      -- Execute BodyPart after establishing Handlers.
```

Figure 4-7: Specification for Conditions package used in Fig. 4-6.

package `Conditions` could be made generic in the type of this data. Of course, there would still be awkwardness if there were several different kinds of data associated with different `Conditions`. An alternative would be to have a single `Conditions` package, *containing* a generic definition of `Signal`:

```
private
   subtype Condition is INTEGER range 1..MaxConditions;
   type ConditionSet is array (Condition) of BOOLEAN;
   OTHERWISE: constant ConditionSet := (Condition => TRUE);
end;  -- Specification part

package body Conditions is
   Number: INTEGER range 0 .. Condition'LAST := 0;
      -- Last Condition value
   subtype FrameType is procedure (C: Condition);
   CurrentFrame: FrameType := begin  null;  end;

   function Init return Condition is
      begin  Number := Number+1;  return Number; end;
   procedure ":="(LHS: out ConditionSet; RHS: Condition) is
      begin LHS := (Condition => FALSE);  LHS[RHS] := TRUE; end;
   -- ":=" on Condition and ConditionSet use the implicit
   -- definitions. "or" on ConditionSet uses the implicit or.
   function ">"(CS: ConditionSet; H: HandlerType) return Assoc is
      begin  return (CS,H);  end;

   procedure Signal(C: Condition) is
      begin  CurrentFrame(C);  end;

   procedure Enable(BodyPart: BodyType; Handlers: HandlerList) is
      LastFrame: constant FrameType := CurrentFrame;
      procedure NewFrame(C: Condition) is
         begin
            CurrentFrame := LastFrame;
            for i in Handlers'RANGE loop
               if Handlers(i).CS(C) then
                  Handlers(i).H(C);
                  CurrentFrame := NewFrame;
                  return;
               end if;
            end loop;
            Signal(C);  -- Pass up the condition.
            CurrentFrame := NewFrame;
         exception
            when others => CurrentFrame := NewFrame; raise;
         end NewFrame;
   begin -- Body of Enable
      CurrentFrame := NewFrame;
      BodyPart;
      CurrentFrame := LastFrame;
   exception
      when others => CurrentFrame := LastFrame; raise;
   end Enable;
end Conditions;
```

Figure 4-8: Implementation of Conditions package specified in Fig. 4-7.

```
package Conditions is
   ...
   generic
      type Data is private;
      ":=": Data'ASSIGN_TYPE := <>;
   package Signaler is
      procedure Signal(C: Condition; X: Data);
      function SignalData return Data;
         -- Return X from latest Signal.  Error if not executing
         -- Signal.
   ...
```

Within a handler, a programmer could have a call on the procedure `SignalData` (which would fail if an appropriate `Signal` was not in progress) to get the data passed to the last `Signal`. The implementation of this is straightforward, involving a global variable to hold the value returned by `SignalData`, and we won't go into any more detail here. Such a practice—using a global variable to pass a parameter—would be open to considerable criticism if it were something a programmer coded explicitly. However, the use of a global variable here, being hidden inside a relatively small package that has exclusive access to it, is acceptable.

To summarize, the various examples in this section illustrate the use of procedure values to define a control structure—the resumable signal—that usually has to be built in to a typical von Neumann-style programming language if it is to appear at all. As the feature is a useful one, we see that what we have done is to make a particular class of language extension largely unnecessary by providing appropriate definitional tools.

4.5 Tasking

It is, perhaps, surprising at first that reviewers within the Department of Defense were willing to accept Ada's tasking model. It requires a considerable re-orientation, after all, to change from a world consisting of processes, shared variables, interrupts, timers, and semaphores (or perhaps processors and messages) to a world consisting of tasks and rendezvous.

This latter world is by no means bad, being in the line of such work as Hoare's Communicating Sequential Processes, but it is a little surprising, given the audience, that such a pre-emptive, unfamiliar, and somewhat complex design was deemed suitable, despite its merits.

A large part of the reason was probably that the competing design (the RED language [Nestor 79]), though at its heart elegant and spare (involving procedure-like processes and "mailboxes"—buffered FIFO queues—for synchronization and communication), was festooned with features to make it livable that had the side-effect of making it appear complex. However, there was also recognition that Ada's tasking provided very useful structure and functionality.

But this still leaves the question of whether we can have our features and eat them, too. Can we derive the benefits of being able to write high-level descriptions of our multi-processing applications without having to build in a tasking facility such as Ada's? Can we get the same effect using a simple and familiar set of primitives and the appropriate abstraction mechanism? Can we formulate all this as a set of packages that need not be standard parts of the language? As we shall see, the answer to all these questions is yes.

4.5.1 Review of features that must be captured

An Ada task is a combination of monitor—a protector of shared data—and process—an executor of statements. The bodies of **accept** statements may be viewed as monitor routines, which are executed in mutual exclusion. These routined are imbedded in text that serves both as a *regular path expression* [Campbell 74]—specifying the order in which these routines may be executed by other processes—and as an independently process in its own right. The design decision to imbed **accept** bodies in the text of the task somewhat obscures the monitor/path expression side of Ada tasking, while the design to follow will, in contrast, emphasize it. Therefore, a short example might be useful at this point.

Consider a simple case of a task with two mutually exclusive entries, as shown in Fig. 4-9. A more traditional (monitor-like) arrangement would be to write the **accept** bodies as procedures, as shown in Fig. 4-10. In this figure, the executable part of ReadWrite is a regular path expression, a more concise form of which is the regular expression

$$(\text{Read} + \text{Write})^*$$

indicating zero or more mutually exclusive occurrences of Read and Write[41]. The path expression serves to synchronize reading and writing. This ordering is trivial, but in general the ordering could include conditional expressions and an arbitrarily complex control structure.

```
task type ReadWrite is
   entry Read(x: out T);
   entry Write(x: T);
end ReadWrite;

task body ReadWrite is
   data declarations
begin
   loop
      select
         accept Read(...) do body of Read end;
      or accept Write(...) do body of Write end;
      end select;
   end loop;
end;
```

Figure 4-9: Simple exclusive Read and Write in Ada.

The Ada tasking mechanism, then, consists of

- A way of creating independently-executing processes (possibly dynamically).

---

[41] Well, the task body as written requires an infinite number of occurrences, but let's ignore that here.

```
task body ReadWrite is
    data declarations

    entry Read(...) is begin body of Read end;
    entry Write(...) is begin body of Write end;

begin
    loop select
        accept Read; or accept Write;
    end select;  end loop;
end
```

Figure 4-10: Example of Fig. 4-9 with **accept** bodies pulled out.

- A method of referring to individual processes as objects (task variables).

- A method of specifying a procedural interface to these processes in the form of a set of monitor routines that are exported by the process, and that may be executed in mutual exclusion among themselves under control of (and synchronously with) the process.

- A method, within each process, of indicating a set of eligible routines and of waiting for the execution of one of them.

- A set of features for waiting for all tasks defined in a block to finish.

- Various features for aborting tasks, asynchronously raising exceptions, and specifying time-outs.

In the next section, we will try to capture these points in an ordinary Ada package. In the process, we will actually create a very useful generalization of the task specification. While the result may not be, perhaps, as aesthetically pleasing as the built-in syntax, it will distribute information in the same way and provide the same functionality.

4.5.2 Unadorned tasks

Let's consider first the "unadorned" task—i.e., a task with no entries. In current Ada, we write

```
task Performer;

task body Performer is
   declarations
begin statements end;
```

There are now certain operations and inquiries available on `Performer`: **abort** `Performer`, **raise** `Performer'FAILURE`, `Performer'TERMINATED`, and the implicit wait for termination that occurs upon exit from the block declaring it.

The body of `Performer` looks for all the world like a procedure, which suggests that we can create a set of definitions that allow us to write

```
Performer: Task :=
   declare
      declarations
   begin statements end;
```

where the type `Task` has such operations as `ABORT` defined on it. (In calling it "`Task`", of course, I am optimistically assuming that we will make the keyword **task** go away.) Figure 4-11 exhibits just such a set of definitions.

4.5.3 Implementation issues with unadorned tasks

It goes without saying that in the absence of built-in tasks, the package in Fig. 4-11 cannot be implemented directly in our proposed Ada without some external support—machine language subprograms and the like. There is no reason to think that such support would be any more complex than what would have to be built into the run-time system in current Ada. Regardless of what sort of external support we use, however, there is some question as to how many "hooks" would have to be present in the run-time system so that the body of `Tasking1` could have sufficient information and control to do its job.

```
package Tasking1 is
   type Task is private;
      -- A Task object, T, is an independently executing
      -- procedure. Initially, IsActive(T) (q.v.) is FALSE.  It
      -- may be activated once by assignment of a
      -- procedure to execute.
   type TaskId is private;
      -- Each task has an Id of type TaskId.
   type TaskList is array (INTEGER range <>) of TaskId;

   procedure ":="(LHS: out TaskId; RHS: TaskId);
   procedure ":="(LHS: out TaskId; RHS: Task);
      -- Post-condition: LHS contains the Id of RHS.  Allows use
      -- of Task variables as arguments that must be TaskIds.
   procedure ":="(LHS: in out Task; RHS: procedure);
      -- Make RHS the body of LHS and begin execution, so that
      -- IsActive(LHS). Illegal if LHS has been activated
      -- previously.
   -- N.B. There is no assignment of Tasks to Tasks.

   procedure ABORT(L: TaskList);
   function IsActive(T: TaskId) return BOOLEAN;
   procedure JOIN(L: TaskList);
      -- Wait until all members of L are no longer active.
   -- It is illegal to leave a block containing active Task
   -- objects until all are terminated.
end Tasking1;
```

Figure 4-11: Simple tasking package.

Basically, the implementation of our tasking package will have to be able to get hold of the execution stack and any other global variables used by the run-time system, such as any frame pointer used by the exception handler and free-list pointers used by the heap storage allocator. It would be useful to be able to trap block exits—that is, to be able to request that the run-time system notify a certain module whenever a block is to be exited, or a certain type of object de-allocated. It is probably possible to "kludge" this in any particular implementation without having to touch the run-time system, using such tricks as replacing the return pointer in a stack frame with a pointer that causes return to a special routine (allowing the implementor to trap subprogram exits). This is a risky approach, however, and one would hope to do better.

A much safer approach is possible if the run-time system itself is constructed with abstraction principles in mind. Suppose that the Ada run-time support for a particular implementation is cast as a special package that contains implementations of the operations of some abstract machine. These operations include such things as block entry and exit routines, and may consist of in-line code or closed procedures. In generating code, a compiler would refer to this package. To support particularly exotic packages, the implementor could supply a new implementation of this package, perhaps containing additional routines. Though this topic is intriguing, it is beyond the scope of this thesis[42].

```
task type Buffer is
   entry Read(x: out T);
      -- Remove next available element from queue and put in x.
   entry Write(x: T);
      -- Place x in queue (when there is room)
end Buffer;

B1: Buffer;

task body Buffer is
   queue data declarations
   SIZE: INTEGER range 0 .. MaxElements := 0;
begin
   loop
      select
         when SIZE>0 =>
            accept Read(x: out T) do
               remove element from queue and place in x;
               SIZE := SIZE - 1;
            end;
      or when SIZE < MaxElements =>
            accept Write(x: T) do
               place x on queue;
               Size := SIZE + 1;
            end;
      end select;
   end loop;
end Buffer;
```

Figure 4-12: Simple shared bounded buffer in current Ada

[42] I am indebted to Bob Balzer of ISI for suggesting this idea to me.

4.5.4 Adding synchronization

The next step is synchronization. One possibility, of course, is to simply provide semaphores and then leave it to the programmer to "roll his own" synchronization schemes in the (by now) classic manner. Such an approach has the advantage of simplicity for the implementor. For the programmer, it lacks a measure of protection that Ada provides: Because the tasking mechanism in Ada has cognizance of synchronization in progress, it can allow somewhat more graceful recovery from some sorts of disastrous error than might otherwise be possible. For example, a task that is waiting for another task to process a request could be notified that this other task has terminated, rather than having to hang on an abandoned semaphore. Let's see what can be done, therefore, to retain Ada's current high-level communication structure.

As a concrete example, consider a simple finite buffered queue, whose realization in current Ada is shown in Fig. 4-12. We cannot (as usual) get quite as notationally neat a solution in our proposed Ada, but we can get a scheme that distributes information in the same way. Figure 4-13 shows a use of the proposed Ada to implement the bounded buffer. We no longer directly address a task, but rather an *interface* to it. Note that we could have any number of `Buffer` interfaces, each provided by a different kind of task, or perhaps not by a task at all.

Figures 4-14 and 4-15 give package specifications that support the notation used in Fig. 4-13. Actually, because a good implementation of tasking requires considerable interaction between the bodies of these two specifications, the specifications for `Path` would probably be imbedded in `Tasking2`. I have separated the two for the sake of readability.

```
type Buffer is
   record
      Read: procedure (x: out T);
      Write: procedure (x: T);
   end record;

package BufferTasks is new InterfacedTask(Buffer);
B1Task: BufferTasks.Task :=
   declare
      type PathNames is (R,W);
      package BufferPath is new Path(PathNames);
      use BufferPath;
      queue data declarations
      SIZE: INTEGER range 0 .. MaxElements := 0;

      procedure Read(x: out T) is begin
         REGION(R,
            begin
            remove element from queue and place in x;
            SIZE := SIZE - 1;
            end);
         end;
      procedure Write(x: T) is begin
         REGION(W,
            begin
            place x on queue;
            Size := SIZE + 1;
            end);
         end;

   begin
      SetInterface(Buffer'(Read,Write));

   -- Path expression
      loop
         SELECT( (SIZE>0, R) or (SIZE<MaxSize, W) );
      end loop;
   end;

B1: constant Buffer := Interface(B1Task);
```

Figure 4-13: Use of tasks with interfaces to get bounded Buffer type

4.6 Summary

This chapter has dealt with the interaction—the mutual support—of two of the criteria listed in section 1.3—the expressiveness of definitional constructs and the simplication of a language that results when its abstraction facilities are general enough to encompass what would otherwise be individual "features." We saw how a class of data types—the fixed-point numeric types

```
package Tasking2 is
   type TaskId is private;
      -- Each task has an Id of type TaskId.
   type TaskList is array (INTEGER range <>) of TaskId;

   procedure ":="(LHS: out TaskId; RHS: TaskId);

   procedure ABORT(L: TaskList);
   function IsActive(T: TaskId) return BOOLEAN;
   procedure JOIN(L: TaskList);
      -- Wait until all members of L are no longer active.
   -- It is illegal to leave a block containing active Task
   -- objects until all are terminated.

   generic
      type InterfaceType is private;
      ":=": InterfaceType'ASSIGN_TYPE := ":=";
   package InterfacedTask is
      type Task is private;
         -- A Task object, T, is an independently executing
         -- procedure. Initially, IsActive(T) (q.v.) is FALSE.
         -- T may be activated once by assignment of a
         -- procedure to execute.

      procedure ":="(LHS: out TaskId; RHS: Task);
         -- Post-condition: LHS contains the Id of RHS.  Allows
         -- use of Task variables for TaskIds.
      procedure ":="(LHS: in out Task; RHS: procedure);
         -- Make RHS the body of LHS and begin execution, so that
         -- IsActive(LHS). Illegal if LHS has been activated
         -- previously.

      procedure SetInterface(I: InterfaceType);
         -- The value of Interface(T), for T the current task,
         -- becomes I.
      function Interface(T: Task) return InterfaceType;
         -- Return the last value supplied by SetInterface
         -- within T.  Wait, if necessary, for it to be set by T.
   end InterfacedTask;
end Tasking2;
```

Figure 4-14: Specifications for tasks with interfaces

—could be defined as ordinary private types rather than being wired into the syntax (and to every implementation) of Ada. To achieve the same notational convenience as current Ada, we needed only a slight generalization of the assignment operator. We also saw how a class of *control* abstractions—tasks—could be formulated, given an appropriate tool, a generalized version of the generic procedure parameter. Again, these generalizations were bought at no particular cost at execution time.

```
generic
   type IdType is private;
   Ord: function (x: IdType) return INTEGER := IdType'ORD;
   First: IdType := IdType'FIRST;
   Last: IdType := IdType'LAST;
      -- The Ord of every value of (sub)type IdType must be in
      -- in the range Ord(First) .. Ord(Last)
package Path is
-- Each instantiation of Path embodies a predicate path
-- expression defined by calls on the routines below.  Each
-- action on the path is identified by a member of IdType.  The
-- programmer uses the REGION procedure to associate members of
-- IdType with particular bodies of code.  Other subprograms
-- indicate which actions are allowed at any particular time.

   subtype Body is procedure;
   procedure REGION(Id: IdType; ProtectedRegion: Body);
      -- ProtectedRegion is executed as allowed by the path.

   type PredicatedAction is
      record  Predicate: BOOLEAN; Action: IdType;  end record;
   type Choice is array (NATURAL range <>) of PredicatedAction;
   subtype OneChoice is Choice(1..1);
   procedure ":="(LHS: in out OneChoice; RHS: PredicatedAction);
      -- LHS becomes (1 => RHS)
   procedure ":="(LHS: in out OneChoice; RHS: IdType);
      -- Same as LHS := PredicatedAction'(TRUE, RHS)
   function "or"(x,y: Choice) return Choice;
      -- Returns concatenation of x and y.

   procedure ACCEPT(Id: IdType);
      -- Specifies the one-element path Id.
   procedure SELECT(C: Choice);
      -- Specifies selection of one of the action specified by
      -- one of the PredicatedActions whose predicate is TRUE.
   function LastAction return IdType;
      -- Returns the Id of the last action taken.
      -- Erroneous before first ACCEPT or SELECT.
   function COUNT(Id: IdType) return INTEGER;
      -- Return number of instantaneously active REGION calls
      -- that specify Id, but have not yet been accepted.

end Path;
```

Figure 4-15: Specification for path expression type

Chapter 5
Conclusions

A programming language is composed of two main parts: a notational and definitional framework, and a set of primitive definitions. This thesis considered the former, making a qualitative study of the effects of generalizing the definitional mechanisms of a particular language on the complexity and expressive power of that language and on the expected performance of programs written in that language. By "complexity" in this context, I refer to two things:

- The number of concepts in the language.

- The amount of semantics that are an essential, primitive part of the language—that cannot be factored out and placed in a "standard prelude" or (preferably) standard library, and that cannot be defined within the rest of the language with only small and well-controlled assists from outside the language, such as machine code.

The phrase "expressive power" refers not to the set of possible input-output behaviors of programs, but rather to

- The programmer's ability to express, in one place, a design decision whose implementation must be distributed throughout the statements of a program. I have called this "incrementality"—the ability to define something once and thereafter build upon it.

- The programmer's ability to communicate intent to the translator.

In Chapters 2 and 3, we saw how deficiencies in the definitional mechanisms of Preliminary Ada hurt its utility as a programming tool unnecessarily—by limiting the composition of private or record types, by making the use of tasks as data objects clumsy—and also affected the performance of its implementations—by not allowing the programmer to give the compiler enough information concerning the use of parameters or the extent of task objects.

Chapter 4 then considered the expected effects of more substantial changes to the current version of the Ada language. There we saw that derived types, which are a source of considerable complexity in the language design, were unnecessary; and that with the addition of two definitional mechanisms, several entire sections of the language—approximate arithmetic, tasking, generic definitions—could be removed or separated out into library packages. Furthermore, these new mechanisms—the assignment operator and the subprogram type—do not require any particular sacrifice of run-time performance

I suspect that many researchers in the field, especially those in academia, will find these results quite obvious and entirely expected: hardly worth raising a fuss over, in fact. But this "common knowledge," if it exists, seems not to have affected the sorts of programming languages that programmers outside academia seem to request or design. Almost all critiques of the Ada language that I have seen proceed from the premise that if a certain feature is not built into the language, it will never be possible to satisfactorily achieve its effect; that the inefficiencies or notational inconvenience of using a simple definitional framework must necessarily frustrate any attempt at adequately defining that feature. Thus, the success of Lisp as an example of how a relatively simple definitional framework can support a whole range of extensions and specializations is considered irrelevant because Lisp is seen as buying its power at the expense of performance. A main theme of this thesis is that abstraction mechanisms do not involve the costs that are popularly supposed.

5.1 Future Research

One obvious next step is to implement a version of the language proposed in this thesis, and to compare the size of the implementation, the quality of the code produced, and the effects on programmer productivity with those for current Ada. One compelling reason for not doing that in this thesis is that there is at present no suitable Ada compiler to use for comparison.

Actually, the language revisions proposed in Chapter 4 were less radical than they might have been simply because I was interested in showing the effects of small changes in the language. It would be interesting to see the effects of a truly radical change that left very little *except* a definitional framework.

This thesis certainly came nowhere near exhausting the possible definitional "hooks" one can build into a language. For example, the ability to specify arbitrary procedures for initializing or de-allocating ("finalizing") a variable is a feature of such languages as Alphard. It provides one more way to hide the implementation of variables of a given type from the users of that type. The utility of such extensions is another area that might be explored.

In Section 4.5.3, there was a passing mention of a technique for presenting the run-time system to the compiler (and systems programmer) as a form of Ada package, allowing the easy re-implementation or augmentation of such things as subprogram entry, exception raising, or variable allocation. An obvious question is how successful such an approach can be. First, there is the issue of how one specifies such a package, and to what extent its specification can be made independent of implementation. If one takes this approach, there is less that a compiler can assume about the run-time support, which raises the question of how this strategy affects optimization. There is finally the issue of how safe such an approach can be—whether the package can be designed to avoid obscure interactions among its definitions.

One part of the suggestions made in this thesis have to do with re-formulating parts of the language definition as packages. This allows one to build smaller compilers and offers greater flexibility in defining these parts of the language, of course, but in a sense it trades one problem for an equal one. The art of designing library packages is not very well developed at the moment. I cannot claim that the definitions offered in Chapter 4 were any more than a feasibility proof, and it would be instructive to explore alternative definitions for the facilities considered.

5.2 A Closing Thought on Simplicity

The original motivation behind this thesis was a challenge that was put to me after an informal talk where I had been discussing differences between Preliminary Ada and Revised Ada. My questioner averred that he found it unbelievable that the art of language design had advanced so little that it should still involve wading through such an apparent morass of detail. This question put me in a somewhat delicate position. On the one hand, I agreed with the spirit of the question, and still think that Ada could have been semantically neater. On the other hand, I also thought that the objection raised by this question was out-weighed by the benefits to be gained by bringing a high-level language such as Ada into common use in applications currently served by much more primitive tools, and therefore I did not feel free at the time to heartily agree with the objection. Clearly, though, this was purely a political reservation on my part, and this thesis is an attempt to address the issue from a purely technical point of view.

In doing so, I have come to the conclusion that simplicity *per se* is not really an issue. A view that has been expressed by as prominent an authority as C. A. R. Hoare (in his Turing Award address [Hoare 81]) is that Ada as it stands is dangerously complex and that what is really needed is a much stripped-down subset, containing just those features that will be used in every application. I believe that this view is naive, or at least insufficiently specific. In its most extreme form it would have us programming Turing machines to implement programs specified in the pure first-order predicate calculus. Such complexity as we leave out of the language will get introduced in another form —as the set of packages, pre-processors, etc., that make the language livable. After all, the various features that are currently wired into the Ada language are not entirely arbitrary, but for the most part represent things that will be used and therefore must be implemented by someone.

Therefore, although I believe simplicity of compilers and of language design to be distinct advantages of the definitional approach advocated in this thesis, I still see the primary advantages of the approach to be in what it adds rather than in what it allows us to eliminate. A programming language, after all, is a relatively fixed target; to a certain extent, its complexity is mitigated by the fact that it sits still for us to learn it. What is really important is our ability to incrementally build programming environments around these languages. It is in this task that definitional mechanisms have their most important application.

Appendix A
Summary of Proposed Revisions to Ada

The following is a list of the various changes proposed in Chapter 4.

Derived types and numeric types

1. Remove derived type definitions. Remove integer type definitions and floating point type definitions, leaving only the predefined type definitions.

Assignment

2. Remove the **limited** keyword and instead make all private types "limited" in the sense that they do not automatically export a ":=" or "=" operator.

3. Add ":=" as a definable binary operator and make the operator "=" an ordinary relational operator in all respects, eliminating the current restrictions on its argument and return types, in particular. The operator ":=" must be a procedure with two operands. It is treated as an ordinary binary operator having lowest precedence. An invocation

   ```
   A := B;
   ```

   is equivalent to

   ```
   ":="(A,B);
   ```

4. Define the operators ":=", "=", and "/=" implicitly on all scalar and access types, as in the current semantics. Likewise, define an implicit ":=" operator on any array or record type for which there is an ":=" operator visible for each component's type.

These are component-wise assignments using the assignment operators defined on the components. They behave as in current Ada with respect to discriminants and index constraints.

5. An invocation of a ":=" operator is type-valid (i.e., is legal within the type system) if its two actuals have the same types as their corresponding formals. An invocation of any other subprogram is type-valid if each actual parameter has the same type as the corresponding formal or is *assignment compatible* with the formal. A parameter is assignment compatible if it is an **in** parameter and there is a unique ":=" operator visible at the point of call with the formal's type as the type of its left operand and the actual's type as the type of its right operand.

6. Unconstrained formal parameters inherit any discriminant constraints as in current Ada, except in the (formerly illegal) case where an unconstrained **in** parameter does not have the same type as its actual. In this case, the discriminants of the formal are set by the assignment operator.

7. Because of rule 8. , some parameters to the assignment operator will have constraints that were formerly impossible—e.g., **in out** array parameters in which the actual parameter does not have an index constraint. As an implementation restriction, any such parameter may only be assigned to in the body of the assignment operator.

9. Parameters are passed to the ":=" operator by reference. Any constraints on the formals must equal those of the actuals. For other subprograms, parameters that are assignment compatible, but not of equivalent type, are copied by the appropriate assignment operator (which must be visible at the point of call). Parameters that are of equivalent type may be passed by copy, using any assignment operator with the correct parameter types visible at either the call site or subprogram body. Parameters that

are of equivalent type and constraints may be passed by reference. (These last two cases are just the extension of current Ada's ambiguity regarding passing by reference vs. passing by value).

10. Outside the package containing it, an operator designator is always visible throughout its scope according to the rules for identifiers made visible by a **use** clause.

11. An explicit definition of ":=" within a package overrides any implicit definition of ":=" introduced by the full type declaration for the private type. For a type T, the notation T'ASSIGN is a synonym for any implicit assignment operator originally defined on it.

12. Do not extend "=" automatically to array or record types, but define it on the pre-defined type STRING.

13. Invoke the ":=" operator implicitly to initialize a variable or constant, to copy a value into an aggregate, and to copy an initial value into a record component.

Literals

14. There is a pre-defined type in STANDARD declared

```
type NUMERIC_LITERAL is
   array (NATURAL range <>) of CHARACTER;
```

Any numeric_literal, N, occurring in program text is equivalent to the aggregate NUMERIC_LITERAL'("N").

15. Any pre-defined numeric types have ":=" operators defined going from NUMERIC_LITERAL to the numeric type that provide the necessary literals.

16. To make qualification work as before, we'll say that if a qualified

expression T'(E) is used as a value then it is valid if (E) can be interpreted as a T or if it is assignment compatible with T.

Fixed point types

17. Remove fixed point types. Their affect can be attained through a package.

Subprogram types

18. The syntax for type_mark is changed to

    type_mark ::= *type*_name | *subtype*_name
                  | subprogram_type

19. A subprogram_type is essentially a subprogram specification, slightly modified:

    subprogram_type ::=
      procedure [formal_part]
      | **function** [formal_part] **return** subtype_indication

20. The operation ":=" is defined implicitly on each functional type, but "=" is not. The effect of the assignment is to make the assigned-to variable refer to the subprogram value of the right operand, but with parameter names and default values as given for the declaration of the left operand. This same replacement of parameter names and default values occurs to a subprogram value returned as the result of a function call.

21. A named constant of a subprogram type may be deferred, just as can a constant of a private type. A complete definition must appear later in the same declarative part (where, for this purpose, the body and private part of a package are considered to be in the same declarative part as the visible part).

22. The literals of a subprogram type are unlabeled blocks:

```
subprogram_constant ::=
        [declare
           declarative_part]
        begin
           sequence_of_statements
        [exception
           {exception_handler} ]
        end
```

The same block may designate subprograms of several different subprogram types. The type must be determined from surrounding context, without reference to the text of the literal. Any free variables in the subprogram constant are bound in the context in which the constant is elaborated (i.e., not at the point the subprogram denoted is eventually called). Note that the rules stated so far combine with existing parts of the language to provide fully qualified subprogram constants (what a Lisp programmer would call lambda expressions), as in

```
function (x: INTEGER) return INTEGER'(begin return x+1; end)
```

which denotes the successor function on the type INTEGER.

23. The declaration

```
procedure identifier [ formal_part ] is
      declarative_part
begin
   . . .
end [ designator ];
```

is an alternate form of

```
identifier: constant procedure [ formal_part ] :=
            declare
               declarative_part
            begin
               . . .
            end [ designator ];
```

and likewise for functions.

24. Two instances of subprogram_type denote the same type if the

sequence of subtypes of the formal parts (in order) are pairwise identical, and the return types, if any, denote the same subtype.

25. Calling a subprogram object that has an assigned value proceeds as does a call in current Ada. Calling a subprogram object without a defined value raises an exception (`UNDEFINED_SUBPROGRAM`). As in current Ada, names of subprogram objects may be overloaded and resolved by context.

26. It is illegal to call a subprogram value when an object referenced in that subprogram value has been de-allocated.

27. Subprogram designators (such as "+") are legal as identifiers in object declarations (allowing, e.g.,

```
":=" : procedure (x: out T; y: T);)
```

Generics

28. The syntax for generic_formal_parameter becomes

```
generic_formal_parameter ::=
    parameter_declaration;
  | identifier_list: [in] subtype_indication := <>;
  | type identifier [discriminant_part]
      is generic_type_definition;
```

Generic parameters having a default value specified "<>" that are left unspecified in a generic instantiation are replaced by the value of a visible object with the same identifier in the instantiating context (if one exists and is unique).

Tasking

29. Remove tasking, supplying it as a package where needed.

Appendix B
Interesting Examples of the Use of Ada

During the course of my work on Ada, I stumbled across several interesting programs and programming techniques that are peripheral to the principal theme of this thesis, but which I simply could not bear to leave unprinted. The strong-stomached reader will find them below.

B.1 Dimensional Analysis in Ada

As indicated in Section 4.1.2.3, Ada's derived type mechanism does not of itself provide a facility for doing true dimensional analysis. It is possible, however, to define a package that does a fairly good job of it. The idea and the original version of the packages below come from unpublished notes by John Nestor. This original version was written in the RED language [Nestor 79].

First a little background: The term *dimensional analysis* here refers to the checking of expressions involving various measurements to make sure that the units of the results match those of the destinations of those results. For example, a computation that is supposed to yield an area (units of length squared), may not consist of adding two lengths (which would yield a length), nor of dividing a length by a duration (which would yield a velocity). The rules of dimensional analysis should be fairly familiar. The paper by Karr and Loveman [Karr 78] gives further details.

The package `UNITS1` in Fig. B-1 allows the programmer to work with up to three incommensurable units (a common triplet is mass, distance, and time).

This first version of the package only checks for agreement of dimension, and requires that the programmer keep track of scaling factors (units of measure) for himself. Figure B-2 shows the private part and body of the package. Both specification and body are written entirely in current Ada.

```
package UNITS1 is

   type UNIT(d1,d2,d3: INTEGER) is private;
      -- The three basic units of measure have subtypes
      -- UNIT(1,0,0), UNIT(0,1,0), and UNIT(0,0,1).
      -- If we let these be called a's, b's, and c's,
      -- then UNIT(d1,d2,d3) represents the subtype of the
      -- composite unit equivalent to a^d1 b^d2 c^d3.

-- The following operators treat UNITs as if they were FLOATs,
-- but raise CONSTRAINT_ERROR exception in case of
-- dimensional conflict.

   function "+"(x,y: UNIT) return UNIT;
   function "+"(x: UNIT) return UNIT;
   function "-"(x,y: UNIT) return UNIT;
   function "-"(x: UNIT) return UNIT;
   function "*"(x,y: UNIT) return UNIT;
   function "/"(x,y: UNIT) return UNIT;
   function "**"(x: UNIT; y: INTEGER) return UNIT;
   function "*"(x: FLOAT; y: UNIT) return UNIT;
   function "*"(x: UNIT; y: FLOAT) return UNIT;
   function "/"(x: FLOAT; y: UNIT) return UNIT;
   function "/"(x: UNIT; y: FLOAT) return UNIT;

   function Unitize(x: FLOAT; y: UNIT) return UNIT;
      -- Converts x to a UNIT value with same dimension as y.
      -- Value of y is ignored.
   function Val(x: UNIT) return FLOAT;
      -- Returns the numeric value of x. Val(Unitize(x,y)) = x.
```

Private part

```
end UNITS1;
```

Figure B-1: Specifications for simple dimensional-analysis package (in current Ada).

Suppose, for example, that we will be dealing with measurements in CGS units. We might define

```
subtype cm is UNIT(1,0,0);
subtype gm is UNIT(0,1,0);
subtype sec is UNIT(0,0,1);
subtype erg is UNIT(2,1,-2);   -- gm cm²/sec²

L1,L2: cm;
M: gm;
T: sec;
E: erg;
```

Now the expressions L1+L2 and M * L1**2/ T**2 will yield the appropriate arithmetic results (as if L1, L2, M, T were variables of type FLOAT), and the values of expressions L2 and E*T*T/(M*L2) can both be assigned to L1. However, the expression L + T will raise an exception (CONSTRAINT_ERROR) as will assignment of M to L1.

Note that since all the subtypes in this example are static, and since all subprograms have been declared to be inline, it is feasible for the compiler to remove all run-time computation of dimensionality, as well as all checking code. Furthermore, in the case of an expression that will cause a mis-match of dimensions, it is feasible for the compiler to warn of the inevitable exception at translation time.

With the revisions to the language sketched in Chapter 4, we can a step further and provide automatic conversion of units. That is, we can allow the programmer to declare that a certain variable has units of inches and that another has units of centimeters, and have the program perform any necessary conversions automatically (still requiring dimensional consistency). To do so, we include a scaling factor (type FLOAT) among the discriminants of the type UNIT and re-define ":=" to takes into account the possibility of differing units in its right and left operands. As long as we re-define ":=", we can also create a new exception, DIMENSION_ERROR to distinguish errors involving incompatible dimensionality more precisely. Figure B-3 shows a set of specifications for the new facility, and Fig. B-4 shows an implementation.

```
private
   type UNIT(d1,d2,d3: INTEGER) is
      record  V: FLOAT; end record;
   pragma INLINE("+","-","*","/","**",Unitize);
end UNITS1;

package body UNITS1 is
   procedure Check(x,y: UNIT) is
      begin
      if x.d1 /= y.d1 or x.d2 /= y.d2 or x.d3 /= y.d3
         then raise CONSTRAINT_ERROR;
      end if;
      end Check;
   pragma INLINE(Check);

   function "+"(x,y: UNIT) return UNIT is
      begin
         Check(x,y);
         return (x.d1,x.d2,x.d3,x.V + y.V);
      end;
   function "+"(x: UNIT) return UNIT is
      begin  return x;  end;
   function "-"(x,y: UNIT) return UNIT is
      begin
         Check(x,y);
         return (x.d1,x.d2,x.d3,x.V - y.V);
      end;
   function "-"(x: UNIT) return UNIT is
      begin  return (x.d1,x.d2,x.d3,-x.V);  end;
   function "*"(x,y: UNIT) return UNIT is
      begin return (x.d1+y.d1,x.d2+y.d2,x.d3+y.d3,x.V*y.V); end;
   function "/"(x,y: UNIT) return UNIT is
      begin return (x.d1-y.d1,x.d2-y.d2,x.d3-y.d3,x.V/y.V); end;
   function "**"(x: UNIT; y: INTEGER) return UNIT is
      begin  return (x.d1*y,x.d2*y,x.d3*y,x.V**y);  end;

   function "*"(x: FLOAT; y: UNIT) return UNIT is
      begin  return (y.d1,y.d2,y.d3,x*y.V);  end;
   function "*"(x: UNIT; y: FLOAT) return UNIT is
      begin  return (x.d1,x.d2,x.d3,x.V*y);  end;
   function "/"(x: FLOAT; y: UNIT) return UNIT is
      begin  return (-y.d1,-y.d2,-y.d3,x/y.V);  end;
   function "/"(x: UNIT; y: FLOAT) return UNIT is
      begin  return (x.d1,x.d2,x.d3,x.V/y);  end;

   function Unitize(x: FLOAT; y: UNIT) return UNIT is
      begin  return (y.d1,y.d2,y.d3,x);  end;
   function Val(x: UNIT) return FLOAT is
      begin  return x.V;  end;

end UNITS1;
```

Figure B-2: Implementation of UNITS1 package in Fig. B-1.

```
package UNITS2 is
   type UNIT(d1,d2,d3: INTEGER; Scale: FLOAT) is private;
      -- The three basic units of measure have subtypes
      -- UNIT(1,0,0,1.0), UNIT(0,1,0,1.0), and UNIT(0,0,1,1.0).
      -- If we let these be called a's, b's, and c's,
      -- then UNIT(d1,d2,d3,s) represents the subtype of the
      -- composite unit equivalent to s · a^d1 b^d2 c^d3 's.

-- In the specifications that follow, assume that x has a subtype
-- of (x1,x2,x3,sx) and y has a subtype of (y1,y2,y3,sy).  The
-- result is always the standard arithmetic result (as for
-- ordinary FLOATing arithmetic, but the scale in which the
-- result appears depends on sx and sy.

   function "+"(x,y: UNIT) return UNIT;
      -- Returns result with units of sx.
   function "+"(x: UNIT) return UNIT;  -- Unary +
   function "-"(x,y: UNIT) return UNIT;
      -- Same result subtype as for "+"
   function "-"(x,y: UNIT) return UNIT;
   function "*"(x,y: UNIT) return UNIT;
      -- Scale of result is sx*sy.
   function "/"(x,y: UNIT) return UNIT;
      -- Scale of result is sx/sy.
   function "**"(x: UNIT; y: INTEGER) return UNIT;
      -- Scale of result is sx**y.
   function "*"(x: FLOAT; y: UNIT) return UNIT;
      -- Scale of result is sy.
   function "*"(x: UNIT; y: FLOAT) return UNIT;
      -- Scale of result is sx.
   function "/"(x: FLOAT; y: UNIT) return UNIT;
      -- Scale of result is 1/sy.
   function "/"(x: UNIT; y: FLOAT) return UNIT;
      -- Scale of result is sx.

   function Unitize(x: FLOAT; y: UNIT) return UNIT;
      -- Val(Unitize(x,y),y.Scale) = x.  Returns x as a UNIT with
      -- same dimensions and scale as y.
   function Val(x: UNIT; Scale: FLOAT := 1.0) return FLOAT;
      -- Returns the numeric value of x, in units of Scale.
   function Scale(x: UNIT; NewScale: FLOAT) return UNIT;
      -- Converts x to units with scale factor of NewScale
      -- (and same dimensions).

   procedure ":="(LHS: out UNIT; RHS: UNIT);
      -- Succeeds as long as subtype of LHS differs from that of
      -- RHS only in Scale (and there is no overflow of the
      -- range of FLOAT from any conversion).
   DIMENSION_ERROR: exception;

private part
end UNITS2;
```

Figure B-3: Expanded UNITS package specification. Handles scaling.

To use the package, we might declare

```
subtype cm is UNIT(1,0,0,1.0);
subtype m  is UNIT(1,0,0,100.0);
subtype in is UNIT(1,0,0,2.54);
subtype gm is UNIT(0,1,0,1.0);
subtype sec is UNIT(0,0,1,1.0);
subtype min is UNIT(0,0,1,60.0);
subtype erg is UNIT(2,1,-2,1.0);
subtype KwH is UNIT(2,1,-2,3.6E13);

xc: cm;   xm: m;   xi: in;
W: gm;
Ts: sec; Tmin: min;
E: erg; Ekwh: KwH;
```

With these declarations, the expression `xc+xm` is valid (yielding a result in centimeters), as is the assignment

```
Ekwh := xc**2 * W/Tmin**2;
```

which converts its result to kilowatt-hours.

B.2 Universal Unions: Taking the starch out of strong typing

Suppose that we have an application that requires us to keep a list of values of homogeneous type. One way to do so, of course, is define a variant record type (a union), and to make our list contain values of that variant type. This is often rather cumbersome, however, and if this list is used in many places throughout a system, it is convenient to be able to have the definition of the list be independent of the set of types of values that are to be stored in it. Of course, we could solve the problem *a fortiori* by using instantiations of the generic function `UNCHECKED_CONVERSION`. To do so directly, however, is to sacrifice a good measure of protection that the type mechanism affords us against using a value as something that it is not.

The package specified in Fig. B-5 allows us to get around this problem by providing a single type, `Universal`, that (abstractly) contains any value that will fit into its representation, and which keeps track of the type of that value, so that it may be used only in the proper contexts. The notion "fits into its

```
private
   type UNIT(d1,d2,d3: INTEGER; Scale: FLOAT) is
      record  V: FLOAT; end record;
   pragma INLINE("+","-","*","/","**",Unitize,":=",Val,Scale);
end UNITS2;

package body UNITS2 is
   procedure Check(x,y: UNIT) is
      begin
      if x.d1 /= y.d1 or x.d2 /= y.d2 or x.d3 /= y.d3
         then raise DIMENSION_ERROR;
      end if;
      end Check;
   pragma INLINE(Check);

   function "+"(x,y: UNIT) return UNIT is
      begin
         Check(x,y);
         return (x.d1,x.d2,x.d3,x.Scale,
            x.V+(y.Scale/x.Scale)*y.V);
      end;
   function "+"(x: UNIT) return UNIT is
      begin  return x;  end;
   function "-"(x,y: UNIT) return UNIT is
      begin
         Check(x,y);
         return (x.d1,x.d2,x.d3,x.Scale,
            x.V-(y.Scale/x.Scale)*y.V);
      end;
   function "-"(x: UNIT) return UNIT is
      begin  return (x.d1,x.d2,x.d3,x.Scale,-x.V);  end;
   function "*"(x,y: UNIT) return UNIT is
      begin
         return (x.d1+y.d1,x.d2+y.d2,x.d3+y.d3,x.Scale*y.Scale,
            x.V*y.V);
      end;
   function "/"(x,y: UNIT) return UNIT is
      begin
         return (x.d1-y.d1,x.d2-y.d2,x.d3-y.d3,x.Scale/y.Scale,
            x.V/y.V);
      end;
   function "**"(x: UNIT; y: INTEGER) return UNIT is
      begin
         return (x.d1*y,x.d2*y,x.d3*y,x.Scale**y,x.V**y);
      end;
```

Figure B-4: Implementation for UNITS2 package (Fig. B-3). Part 1 of 2.

representation," of course, would be difficult to define with absolute precision, but it is unnecessary for us to do so, because in practice, it suffices to say that an exception will be raised if a value does not fit. If each of the various types is an access type—a common case—then all values are liable to be of the same size.

```
function "*"(x: FLOAT; y: UNIT) return UNIT is
   begin  return (y.d1,y.d2,y.d3,y.Scale,x*y.V);  end;
function "*"(x: UNIT; y: FLOAT) return UNIT is
   begin  return (x.d1,x.d2,x.d3,x.Scale,x.V*y);  end;
function "/"(x: FLOAT; y: UNIT) return UNIT is
   begin  return (-y.d1,-y.d2,-y.d3,1.0/y.Scale,x/y.V);  end;
function "/"(x: UNIT; y: FLOAT) return UNIT is
   begin  return (x.d1,x.d2,x.d3,x.Scale,x.V/y);  end;

function Unitize(x: FLOAT; y: UNIT) return UNIT is
   begin  return (y.d1,y.d2,y.d3,y.Scale,x);  end;
function Val(x: UNIT; Scale: FLOAT := 1.0) return FLOAT is
   begin return x.V*(x.Scale/Scale); end;
function Scale(x: UNIT; NewScale: FLOAT) return UNIT is
   begin
      return (x.d1,x.d2,x.d3,NewScale,(x.Scale/NewScale)*x.V);
   end;

procedure ":="(LHS: out UNIT; RHS: UNIT) is
   begin
      if LHS'CONSTRAINED then
         Check(LHS,RHS);
         LHS.V := RHS.V* (RHS.Scale/LHS.Scale);
      else LHS := RHS;
      end if;
   end;

end UNITS2;
```

Figure B-4: Implementation for UNITS2 package (Fig. B-3). Part 2 of 2.

Using the package in Fig. B-5, we can build a list, each of whose elements is of type `Universal`. If we expand our system and wish to add a new kind of element to the list, say type `NewT`, we need not change any of the declarations that give us the list. Instead, we define

```
package UNewT is new Universals(NewT);  use UNewT;
```

We now have assignments that convert back and forth between type `NewT` and `Universal`, and that insure, furthermore, that only values that were originally created from `NewT`s can be assigned back to `NewT`s.

Figure B-6 gives the implementation for `UniversalPackage`. Note that each instantiation of the `Universals` package "signs in" with the parent, taking its identification token from the counter `NextId` in the parent package, `UniversalPackage`.

```
package UniversalPackage is
   type Universal is private;
   type TypeId is private;
      -- Each instantiation of Universals (below) has a unique
      -- TypeId associated with it.

   function TypeOf(x: Universal) return TypeId;
   NullType: constant TypeId;
      -- The initial TypeId for any variable.
      -- Distinct from any Id for an instantiation of Universals.

   ":=": constant TypeId'ASSIGN_TYPE;
   "=": constant TypeId'EQUAL_TYPE;
   ":=": constant Universal'ASSIGN_TYPE;

   generic
      type T is private;
      ":=": constant T'ASSIGN_TYPE := <>;
   package Universals is
      function Id return TypeId;
         -- Id of all values produced by this instantiation.
      procedure ":="(LHS: Universal; RHS: T);
      procedure ":="(LHS: T; RHS: Universal);
   end Universals;
```

Private part

```
end UniversalPackage;
```

Figure B-5: Specifications for universal union type.

```
private
   subtype TypeId is INTEGER;
   NullType: constant TypeId := 0;
   subtype UniversalRep is INTEGER;   -- Pick any type.
   type Universal is
      record
         Id: TypeId := NullType;
         Val: UniversalRep;
      end record;
end UniversalPackage;

package body UniversalPackage is

   NextId: TypeId := 1;

   function TypeOf(x: Universal) return TypeId is
      begin  return x.Id;  end;

-- Assignment and equality implementations are defaulted.

   package body Universals is
      MyId: constant TypeId := NextId;
      function Id return TypeId is
         begin  return MyId;  end;

      function Union is new UNCHECKED_CONVERSION(T,UniversalRep);
      procedure ":="(LHS: Universal; RHS: T) is
         begin  return (MyId,Union(RHS));  end;
      function Sep is new UNCHECKED_CONVERSION(UniversalRep,T);
      procedure ":="(LHS: T; RHS: Universal) is
         begin
            if MyId = RHS.Id then return Sep(RHS.Val);
            else raise CONSTRAINT_ERROR;
            end if;
         end;

   begin
      NextId := NextId+1;
   end Universals;

end UniversalPackage;
```

Figure B-6: Implementation of universal union package (Fig. B-5).

References

[Ada 80] Ada Language Design Team.
Language Study Note 112: Analysis of the Problems of Derived Types—A simplification.
1980.
Internal design notes of the Language Design Team, March 14, 1980.

[Addyman 80] A. M. Addyman.
A Draft Proposal for PASCAL.
SIGPLAN Notices 15(4):1-66, April, 1980.

[Backus 78] J. Backus.
Can Programming be Liberated from the von Neumann Style? A Functional Style and Its Algebra of Programs.
Communications of the ACM 21(8):613-641, August, 1978.

[Campbell 74] R. H. Campbell and A. N. Habermann.
The specification of process synchronization by path expressions.
In Goos, G. and Hartmanis, J. (editor), *Lecture Notes in Computer Science*, pages 89-102. Springer-Verlag, 1974.

[Carlson 80] Wm. E. Carlson.
A Standard Programming Language for Defense Systems.
SIGNAL , March, 1980.

[Dahl 72] O.-J. Dahl, E. W. Dijkstra, and C. A. R. Hoare.
Structured Programming.
Academic Press, 1972.

[Digital 74] *Bliss/11 Programmer's Manual*
Digital Equipment Corporation, Maynard, Mass., 1974.

[DoD 78] U. S. Department of Defense.
Department of Defense Requirements for High Order Computer Programming Languages, "STEELMAN".
U. S. Department of Defense, 1978.

[Geschke 77] C. M. Geschke, J. H. Morris, and E. H. Satterthwaite.
Early Experience with Mesa.
Communications of the ACM 20(8):540-553, August, 1977.

[Habermann 79] A. N. Habermann, D. S. Notkin, and D. E. Perry.
Report on the Use of Ada for the Design and Implementation of Part of Gandalf.
Technical Report CMU-CS-79-135, Carnegie-Mellon University, Computer Science Department, June, 1979.

[Habermann 80] A. N. Habermann and I. R. Nassi.
Efficient Implementation of Ada Tasks.
Technical Report CMU-CS-80-103, CMU, January, 1980.
To appear in TOPLAS.

[Hilfinger 79a] P. N. Hilfinger.
Discriminant Constraints in Ada.
(Ada) Language Issue Report 8, CMU.

[Hilfinger 79b] P. N. Hilfinger.
The Tasking Facility in Ada.
(Ada) Language Issue Report 9, CMU.

[Hoare 74] C. A. R. Hoare.
Monitors: An Operating System Structuring Concept.
Communications of the ACM 17(10):549-557, October, 1974.
See also Erratum in February, 1975 issue.

[Hoare 78] C. A. R. Hoare.
Communicating Sequential Processes.
Communications of the ACM 21(8):666, August, 1978.

[Hoare 81] C. A. R. Hoare.
The Emperor's Old Clothes.
Communications of the ACM 24(2):75-83, February, 1981.

[Honeywell 79] Honeywell, Inc. and Cii Honeywell Bull.
Set of Sample Problems for DOD High Order Language Program, GREEN Solutions.
Honeywell, Inc., 1979.

[Honeywell 80] Honeywell, Inc. and Cii Honeywell Bull.
Reference Manual for the Ada Programming Language.
United States Department of Defense, 1980.

[Ichbiah 79a] J. D. Ichbiah et al.
Rationale for the Design of the ADA Programming Language.
SIGPLAN Notices 14(6B), June, 1979.

[Ichbiah 79b] J. D. Ichbiah et al.
Preliminary Ada Reference Manual.
SIGPLAN Notices 14(6A), June, 1979.

[Jensen 74] K. Jensen and N. Wirth.
PASCAL User Manual and Report.
Springer-Verlag, 1974.

[Karr 78] M. Karr and D. B. Loveman III.
Incorporation of Units into Programming Languages.
Communications of the ACM 21(5):385-391, May, 1978.

[Lampson 77] B. W. Lampson, J. J. Horning, R. L. London, J. G. Mitchell, and G. J. Popek.
Report on the Programming Language Euclid.
SIGPLAN Notices 12(2):1-79, February, 1977.

[Levin 77] R. Levin.
Program Structures for Exceptional Condition Handling.
PhD thesis, Carnegie-Mellon University, April, 1977.

[Mitchell 78] J. G. Mitchell, W. Maybury, and R. Sweet.
Mesa Language Manual
Xerox Corporation, 1978.
CSL-78-1.

[Nassi 80] I. R. Nassi.
Thoughts on Abstraction in Ada.
1980.
Unpublished position paper, February 5, 1980.

[Nestor 79] J. Nestor and M. Van Deusen.
RED Language Reference Manual.
Intermetrics, Inc., 1979.

[Parnas 71] D. L. Parnas.
Information Distribution Aspects of Design Methodology.
In *Proceedings of IFIP Congress*, pages 26-30. IFIP, 1971.
Booklet TA-3.

[Shaw 74] M. Shaw.
Reduction of Compilation Costs Through Language Contraction.
Communications of the ACM 17(5):245-250, May, 1974.

[Shaw 78] M. Shaw, P. Hilfinger, W. A. Wulf.
TARTAN Language Design for the Ironman Requirement: Reference Manual.
SIGPLAN Notices 13(9):36-58, September, 1978.

[Shaw 80] M. Shaw and W. A. Wulf.
Toward Relaxing Assumptions in Languages and Their Implementations.
SIGPLAN Notices 15(3):45-61, March, 1980.

[Wallis 80] P. J. L. Wallis.
External Representations of Objects of User-Defined Type.
ACM Transactions on Programming Languages and Systems 2(2):137-152, April, 1980.

[Wulf 76] W. A. Wulf, R. L. London, and M. Shaw.
An Introduction to the Construction and Verification of Alphard Programs.
IEEE Transactions on Software Engineering SE-2(4):253-265, 1976.

[Wulf 80a] W. A. Wulf.
Trends in the Design and Implementation of Programming Languages.
Computer 13(1):14-25, January, 1980.

[Wulf 80b] W. A. Wulf, M. Shaw, L. Flon, and P. N. Hilfinger.
Fundamental Structures of Computer Science.
Addison-Wesley Publishing Company, 1980.

Index